The Bridge

Connecting the Powers of
Linear and Circular Thinking

Kim Hudson

D1616925

III Clink
Street

Contents

The Bridge

Preface

When I was a young woman, I applied for a job as a federal land negotiator in the Yukon First Nations Comprehensive Land Claim. It was a golden time for land claims negotiations because there were several people involved who had spent many years of their childhood living in a traditional way.

Heading into my interview, I was almost immobilized with fear. This was a serious and controversial government job – and I really wanted it. Having grown up in the Yukon, my love for the place was deep. As a geologist, I had an unconventional interest in finding a more human and broadly beneficial application for my knowledge of mineral potential. For example, I wondered if Indigenous participation in the Yukon's land management and the mineral resource industry could support First Nations in living the best of a traditional and modern lifestyle. I was also curious to see what might happen in Canada if, through a land claim, Yukon First Nations introduced their worldview into today's practices. Back then I was considered naïve. Amusing, but naïve.

Approaching the interview, I gave myself a pep talk. "Stop worrying that you won't say what the Federal Government wants to hear." I decided my best option was to simply be myself. That way, the interviewer and I could learn if we were a good fit. No withholding, no exaggeration, no trying to conform to Federal expectations. With this shift in mindset, I felt myself relax. I could manage just being myself. It was no longer a zero-sum game. Either way, the outcome was going to be positive. If we didn't find a meeting of minds, I was better off turning my efforts elsewhere. If we seemed compatible, it could be a fabulous job.

Feeling much lighter, I picked up the phone for my interview and actually enjoyed the opportunity to discuss treaty negotiation concepts. Leaving fear behind made room for me to find a sense of connection. Curiously, it seemed that my authentic and relaxed approach also inspired a more human interview. I wondered, "Does the mindset we adopt when approaching a situation influence the way people respond to us?"

I know one thing for sure: I got the job, and it was great.

When I worked as a negotiator, I noticed there was something inherent to the human condition that Yukon First Nations seemed to have made central to their way of being in the world, and that Western culture has largely ignored. I felt compelled to give language to this phenomenon, and it was a struggle.

These ideas never left me. I began to see similar themes in many different places: in investigations about why bureaucracies sometimes fail us; in higher personal value being placed on our happiness; in the emergence of a new type of leadership, one that embraces individual empowerment and makes space for vulnerability and difference; and in deeper consideration of what makes the things we do meaningful.

It seemed that calls for new approaches to the big issues of our time were also calls to understand another side of our human potential. Perhaps our slow response to urgent climate change and social media issues, even our fears of artificial intelligence and a future robot takeover, are part of our floundering quests to find a different approach.

Something from my early experience was being mirrored in these paradigm shifts. I spent seven years searching, researching, and reflecting on what I now call linear and circular thinking to give language to what this might be. The juxtaposition of the linear thinking that dominated my geology and federal government work, and the circular thinking I thought I saw in Yukon First Nations, myself, and some proactive businesses and governments, was rich ground for highlighting the nature of these thinking styles.

A model started to emerge for identifying linear and circular thinking, and for supporting movement between them. I was excited when I discovered scientific research that described similar patterns in the human condition. As I kept exploring, business examples of applying new methods, ones that aligned well with circular principles, became more and more frequent. It felt like a tectonic shift was happening.

Since the dawn of the Industrial Age, most Western operating systems have become mechanistic. This includes business structures, education, healthcare, and environmental management. Our human-centred practices continued intuitively in these areas, often invisibly, and more commonly in our personal relationships.

With the invention of social media with its "like" buttons and algorithms, the circular, and more psychological ways we approach the world, found a modern platform, but often in a disconnecting way. It is concerning to see how our psychological make-up is being gamed to increase marketing power and influence politics. We are yet to fully understand the impacts of the tools being used to foster negative circular power around the world, and to understand the positive alternatives.

Never before has there been a greater need to understand the two ways of knowing inherent to being human. We also need to build a bridge between our linear and circular ways of knowing. Standing on this bridge we see the approach required for finding meaning on one side and how to make progress in a chosen direction on the other. *The Bridge* offers a model for viewing perspectives like the innate differences between artists' and scientists' methodologies, along with the importance of both. And Western and Indigenous cultural values may find their unique platforms with a latticework for holding each perspective on its own terms. Finding the optimal times for transactional as compared to reciprocal agreements, the transition from conflict to shared problems, and service leadership rather than command-and-control leadership can all be supported by having a framework for linear and circular thinking.

The Bridge is not an attempt to chronicle the history of the development of two ways of knowing theory. Nor is it a comprehensive review of the applications of two ways of knowing today. *The Bridge* is an introduction to a tool for participating in linear and circular thinking. The examples are chosen for their clarity and ease of remembering, which is why stories are highly favoured.

The Bridge is a model that illuminates a choice between two ways of knowing in any situation. It inspires a pause while we choose the optimal mindset for moving forward. In this profound moment we can step back and see a bigger pattern rather than being reactive.

This framework is more than a cross-cultural tool. No person or organization is completely linear or circular. We are all bridging both every day, even if that process is unconscious. And, each person, community, and organization finds the combination of circular and linear thinking that feels right. Knowing this, we gain the potential to expand and shift toward a balance point that is most effective in any situation. We become more dynamic.

The bridge framework shows us how to adjust our mindset to align with the thinking style another person is using to communicate with us. Or, we can choose to proactively employ a different mode of thinking, to shift the conversation to a more optimal form of engagement.

After my land claims experience, my partner, a Southern Tutchone man, and I had two daughters together, and eventually separated. Being from Southern Tutchone and Celtic backgrounds, my daughters have grown with me as we moved between the two cultures that structure our lives. They often spoke of the difficulties in moving from one worldview to the other and how we needed some kind of a bridge. The foreword that follows is their gift to me and to this book; a glimpse into their experience of living in these two ways of being.

Chapter 1: We Are of Two Mindsets, begins by showing the power of separating out two ways of knowing the world and seeing the inherent beauty in each. I experience them in the news, in podcasts, at conferences, and in conversations in coffee shops. Pretty quickly, I also see how strong the unconscious drive is to revert to a one-world view where the pattern is blurred. When we see and value the distinctions between the two ways of knowing, we can actively protect them. Linear and circular thinking can find their way to operate side-by-side, strong in their individual ways. When they are blended, their unique powers are weakened.

Chapter 2: I've Got a Name, explores how the distinctiveness of each worldview depends on our careful and thoughtful use of language.

Chapter 3: Why Only Two? takes on the question of how there could possibly be only "two ways of knowing" when there are so many individual and collective perspectives.

Chapter 4: Power, looks at the revelations in our understanding of power that emerge when we have language for linear and circular thinking. For example, I became aware that the two modes are functional opposites of each other. Then it struck me that this means they would have different views of power. I was familiar with linear power, but what did circular power look like?

Chapter 5: The Bridge, walks through the triad of operating principles that provide access to linear and circular thinking. With each principle, I offer examples of how it manifests in life. These examples are not meant to be a complete list as the principles can be applied in many ways; they provide a sampling to initiate those delightful "aha" moments of recognition.

When choosing examples from scientific research that illuminated the principles, I was aware that, as Marshall McLuhan revealed, "the medium is the message." Therefore, I have referenced information from objective scientific reports, academic theories, and surveys for those most comfortable with linear thinking. For the dominantly circular thinkers among us, I refer to story-based podcasts, TED talks, movies, and share stories from my own life to present scientific findings and theories. Sometimes composites of several experiences are told in a story to demonstrate a point. These stories do not refer to a specific person or company and the characters are not given surnames.

My insights from my experiences with First Nations are included with permission to respect the gifts I have received as people took the time to share their perspective with me. The understandings I drew from their generosity are my creation and responsibility.

Foreword

Dännch'e? Nitsulla ùúye, kajät ich'e (How are you? My Indian name is Nitsulla). Hello. I am Jesse, the daughter of Kim Hudson and Dave Joe, and the granddaughter of Jessie and Harry Joe, and Buzz and Jan Hudson. I am a citizen of Champagne and Aishihik First Nations and a member of the Crow Clan.

When I was three, I called my grandmothers White Gramma and Brown Gramma. I'm told people were often taken aback but to me they were terms of endearment.

Growing up, I naturally lived in two worlds. It took me a while to realize how different that was from the lives of my school friends. Who knew it isn't typical to spend summer months with family at Klukshu, a fishing village in the Yukon, where we ate when we were hungry, slept when we were tired, and welcomed what each day offered us? Eventually I noticed that none of my friends in Vancouver learned how to clean fish when they were eight. My winters were spent in Vancouver and full of soccer, shopping, school, piano lessons, and elaborate birthday parties. It's wonderful how easy it is to accept such different worlds without question as a kid.

Fast forward to now. As an adult I work in the world between First Nation, Federal, and Territorial governments. I hear again and again how the key to successfully implementing the First Nations' Final Agreements is to have strong relationships. We ultimately need each other to succeed. This means it is important to have deadlines to stay focused and also to respect people by accommodating different capacities and celebrating personal successes together. We cannot be entirely linear or circular if we hope to succeed when working with multiple governments. We need ways to recognize and practice both.

Growing up in two worlds while my mom was developing this book has given me tools to navigate both linear and circular thinking in my career and my life. I have learned how changing the way I think about a situation can help resolve issues.

Hi. I'm Jesse's sister (Andaya), Jamie. We have the same relations so instead I want to talk about what *The Bridge* means to me.

Our Elders taught us to introduce ourselves to new friends by sharing who we are related to. It helps us self-locate ourselves. We acknowledge our grandparents, our parents, our clan, and our nation. During the introductory period of my Indigenous Governance classes, we followed this practice and so many connections and conversations happened: "Oh, I know your grandparents," or, "Oh, I know your family name, are you related to so and so?" We acknowledge our ancestors and family who came before us in order to connect with those around us in the present moment. It is a foundation that helps me know who I am. By acknowledging our place of origin and creating those connections as we go, it feels as if we are never walking a path alone. We start a relationship by bringing people into our circles of connection.

I feel like I've been living with the model for linear and

circular thinking for the past twenty-two years. Given who my parents are, I live between these two worlds every day, constantly with one foot in each world. I used to view this as a weakness, not fully belonging to one worldview. By understanding and giving respect to these two ways of knowing, I've come to realize that I can be someone who learns to bring them together. As a society, we can all learn to benefit from these two kinds of knowledge.

When I am out in the world, working in a linear institution, I see that people often want to be circular, but very few know how to bring that to the work they are doing. For example, reconciliation feels like a buzzword we often hear these days. To me, reconciliation represents the healing process. It happens at various levels: with self, with family, with community, and within a nation. It is best to start with yourself.

I imagine the process begins by acknowledging we have a disconnection. This judgment-free space requires respect, understanding, desire, and communication. From here, we can have conversations that make a real shift in our relations with one another. It is an ongoing process. We are all learning and unlearning as we go through it. I believe we should hold each other up with gratitude for the small incremental changes we are making to shift the relations between Indigenous and non-Indigenous people. Just as reconciliation is a lifelong practice, the bridge for interpreting two ways of knowing has and will continue to affect my life.

Chapter 1
We Are of Two Mindsets

An End to the Blend

Before every decision, there is a micro-pause to make a choice between two frames of mind. It may happen consciously or unconsciously, fast or slow, and be driven by pleasure or pain. However we describe it, there is a moment of choice between two states.

I don't think this is accidental. Something very powerful happens when we have two distinct states to move between. The contrast between them is the simplest way to create energy and balance. We inhale and exhale, walk on two legs, understand electricity as positive and negative charges. Having two states also creates the potential for patterns to form as seen in the contrast between a grey donkey and a black and white zebra.

Similarly, our thoughts stem from two distinct states: a mindset that feels compelled to push back against what might hurt us, and another mindset that seeks to pull in more of what feeds us. Together they give us the ability to preserve and protect our material gains on one hand, and receive and explore new and nourishing concepts on the other. Again, with conscious possession of our two mindsets we can create a pattern, find a state of balance, and enjoy the energy of contrasts.

Most of the time, thinking is like breathing – we just do it. With this functional blindness to the inherent patterns in our thinking the enormous power gained from seeing our two ways of knowing floats away. The secret to seeing and accessing all the potential power of being human is to separate out our two thinking styles. At first this must be done consciously, and it is awkward and clunky. Eventually it becomes second nature.

There are some people with a natural ability to move from one thinking style to the other. I first recognized this when I started as a federal negotiator. The parties to the Yukon Land Claim negotiations had agreed to try a new method coming out of Harvard called the Negotiation Project. It was based on Roger Fisher and William L. Ury's book *Getting to Yes*. As it was explained to me, we saw ourselves shifting from being parties facing off against each other across the table, to being people on the same side of the table facing shared problems. I loved it. As a result, I am always drawn to Ury's work. I marvel at how he faces enormous conflicts with a curious smile, a sparkle in his eye, and a warm sense of humour alongside his remarkably nimble mind. For example, in his TEDx Midwest talk, Ury describes how he found himself in a near-impossible position: namely, attempting to negotiate a truce between Russia and Chechnya in the 1990s, after twenty-one months of intense fighting with the death of over eighty thousand civilians and soldiers. And this was only one stage of a much longer conflict.

The long history of Russian-Chechen conflict began in the 1700s, when Russia maintained a military road and forts through Chechnya, to fulfill its role as the protectorate of Eastern Georgia. Chechens have been rebelling against this Russian threat to their territories ever since.

During a ceasefire in 1994, Ury was tasked with brokering peace between these ancient enemies. The parties met in

The Hague, also the home of the UN International Court of Justice. As the talks began, the vice president of Chechnya seized the floor to deliver a long and bloody description of Russian activity in Chechnya since the 1700s. He concluded by instructing the Russians to just stay in their seats because very soon they were going to be on trial for war crimes.

Then he turned to Ury and challenged him in his role as the facilitator of these talks because of the US's actions in Puerto Rico. (The vice president of Chechnya was referring to that period in the 1800s when Puerto Rico at first welcomed the Americans in the fight to remove the colonial Spaniards. At the point of victory, the Americans claimed Puerto Rico as their prize. Through the Paris Treaty, the Spanish-American War ended, and Puerto Rico became non-voting US territory.)

Ury described what was going through his mind as his suitability as the facilitator was being challenged:

> My mind started racing. Puerto Rico? What do I know about Puerto Rico? I started reacting... But then, I tried to remember to go to the balcony. And then when he paused and everyone looked at me for a response, from a balcony perspective, I was able to thank him for his remarks and say, "I appreciate your criticism of my country and I take it as a sign that we're among friends and can speak candidly to one another."

How remarkable. Even under intense pressure, Ury was able to separate from one worldview – adversarial and fear-driven – and choose a fresh mindset, one focused on appreciation of candid dialogue. Instead of pushing back against what he didn't want (the perception that he had no legitimacy as a facilitator) he chose to connect to what he and the vice president of Chechnya both wanted, namely, frank talks to understand each other's perspectives and enable meaningful negotiations. He went so far as to characterize the participants as friends.

Framing them as friends was a significant choice for Ury to make. It made him much more vulnerable. But I soon saw the value in moving from enemies, lobbing threats at each other in efforts to force change, to friends in a relationship with a shared desire to stop the suffering and bloodshed in Chechnya. Both realities were represented in the room, but it takes a moment of insight to see that they both exist. When we see them both, we gain the power of a choice. That's why Ury "went to the balcony". It means he took the mental space to pause and consciously disengage from one mindset in order to see other options. From this mind-space he could find the more productive alternative.

If we don't see the two distinct options, invisible assumptions take hold like believing that there is only one way to move forward. In some cases, the parties assume different ways forward, despite believing there is only one, which causes frustrations to escalate. One party may need to deal with the emotional foundation of the issue while the other is focused on being rational and making progress. The two head off on their own tracks and can't understand why they are not connecting.

Even if they are in the same thinking mode, an intense pushing match may ensue because they both know that the party that doesn't back down is declared the winner. In this environment, the opportunity for discovering innovative options is not on the table. Also, when solutions are coerced, they often don't last because the party that feels dominated tends to be subversive first chance they get.

The magic happens when we stop unconsciously blending all our thoughts into one complicated process. Instead, we pause to parse out linear from circular thinking styles. Only then can we check our assumptions and see alternatives by expanding the neglected mindset.

"Going to the balcony" meant Ury was able to skilfully shift a hostile pushing match into a shared dialogue – rather than pushing back against each other, the two sides started pulling in more of what they both wanted.

The result was a peace agreement in which the parties vowed not to resolve their conflicts with force, to withdraw some Russian forces, and to continue talking about the Russian-Chechen relationship. These are not the kinds of terms that are achieved through hostile assertions. Although the treaty was short-lived, (perhaps because the implementers were less skilled at shifting their mindsets) lives were saved while it was in place. The big question is, how did Ury do that?

Ury guides us to "go to the balcony" to see that second option. But when we are standing out there on that metaphorical balcony, it is still very hard to know what we are looking at. I think Ury has a natural gift for it. Leadership guru Daniel Goleman is the same. He provides inspiring examples of those moments of choosing a new mindset in his books *Emotional Intelligence* and *Working with Emotional Intelligence*.

Knowing how this is done in our own lives sometimes feels like a chasm we cannot cross. It is clearly a good thing to make the shift, but where's the bridge?

The bridge framework shows us some key access points that allow us to sort linear from circular thinking. It quickly becomes clear that the two ways of knowing are opposites of each other. When the two thinking styles are blended, the pattern is obscured. Put another way, when blended, for every hint of a pattern in one thinking style there is also a contradiction from the other because the two are opposite in nature.

When "going to the bridge", we have a tool for separating out linear and circular thinking. Only then can we can stand between the two modes, and see three broad operating principles within each mode. Recognising them allows us to identify our current thinking mode, and what the second option looks like. Then we can decide the optimal side of the bridge for moving forward.

Every decision we make, every leadership challenge we face, every conflict we hope to resolve, every danger we need to control, every relationship we hope to foster, and every transformation we hope to support starts with decisions around how to navigate our circular and linear thinking.

Linear thinking seeks to preserve and protect the known. As you can imagine, this makes it very difficult for a strongly linear organization to release, change, and expand their fundamental thinking. Usually, it requires a major breakdown of linear systems for circular thinking to take hold. The Portuguese government found itself doing exactly that when they ran out of linear options for addressing their heroin crisis.

In the 1990s, Portugal was facing a massive drug addiction problem linked to its political history. From 1926 to 1974, the country was ruled by Europe's longest running dictatorship. The citizens rose up and removed that government in 1974, but because generations had grown up under a dictatorship, they collectively struggled to figure out how to form a democracy. At the same time, several Portuguese colonies ousted their colonizers, shipping many bureaucrats and soldiers back to Portugal, along with a dazzling assortment of drugs. The struggle to achieve radical change was slow, while unemployment took off like a wildfire. Drugs became the relief of choice. By the early 1990s, it seemed everyone had a friend or a relative with an addiction problem, with one hundred thousand citizens addicted to heroin alone.

Journalist Johann Hari gave a personal and well-researched TED talk on understandings of addiction. In it, he recounts the Portuguese government's efforts to solve their addiction crisis. At first, the government tried to impose deterrents to addiction by using their authority to inflict pain through larger fines and prison time. The addiction problem increased; crime went up, social cohesion declined, and healthcare costs remained crippling. In the face of this demoralizing failure, the government turned to addiction experts, ready to try anything.

The experts were questioning their foundational understandings of addiction. The history of addiction research had gone something like this: a rat in a cage has two bottles of water to choose from, one infused with cocaine and the other just plain water. The rat tries both bottles, and over time, drinks only the cocaine water until its unfortunate demise. From this experiment, behavioural scientists concluded that once cocaine gets into a rat's system, it is like a hook that compels the rat to get more, even though the cocaine will eventually kill it. The assumption was made that people also get hooked and destroy their lives to get more cocaine because the drug overrides their logical decision-making abilities.

In 1990, Bruce Alexander, a researcher at Simon Fraser University, noticed that the cage in the classic addiction experiment contained only the rat and the water bottle (probably to reduce the study variables). He wondered if it might be the rat's choice between a lonely, joyless life with plain water and the temporary euphoria of feeling loved when it chose the cocaine water, that was causing the result. Alexander wanted to see what would happen if a rat was in a playground with slides and cheese, along with other rats for friendship, and, if it played its cards right, sex. He set up his Rat Park study, and in this enlivened environment, the rats had significantly less interest in the cocaine water when plain water was an option. None of them overdosed.

Alexander and other scientists such as Nina Christie concluded that addiction is an adaptation to a loveless environment. The cocaine offers temporary relief from the excruciating feelings of isolation and being unloved, also known as lack of bonding.

João Goulão, the doctor credited with turning around the Portuguese drug addiction problem, said, "People use drugs for one of two reasons – either to potentiate pleasures or to relieve unpleasure." Goulão's team asked politicians, business owners, family members, addicts, and citizens what they wanted more of. The common theme was that they all wanted to feel that they were among good neighbours.

The goal essentially moved from protecting the good citizens from deviant addict behaviour to the more holistic purpose of supporting all citizens in being good neighbours. This shift in mindset changed everything.

In the new Portuguese plan, addiction was decoupled from dangerous activity like drug trafficking (this behaviour remains a crime punishable by jail time). The possession of drugs for personal use is still illegal but decriminalized. If a person is caught with drugs for personal use, they meet with a special panel with the intention of supporting him or her in being a good neighbour. Here a person shares their story and is offered services such as counselling support, awareness of programs that support safe drug use, and employment opportunities. Only when all this fails is treatment mandated or fines and community service considered.

The plan worked surprisingly well. With reliable sources of low-level drugs and needle exchanges, drug use was safer and less subject to negative community judgments. Community life became more inclusive for people who suffered from addictions, as well as for their families.

In essence, leadership made a 180° shift from the previous attempts to force addicts to be more like non-addicted people, to a drive to meet addicted citizens where they are in their lives and find ways to support them in bringing their best selves to their neighbourhoods. This principle of respecting the free choice of individuals and being inclusive was potentially a significant part of the solution.

In a circular thinking world, everyone is seen for their intrinsic worth – not encouraged to become what others want them to be.

The government also recognized that people feel part of a community when they have a job. A good job gives people dignity and a place to go each day to be among co-workers. It also allows them to take pride in their accomplishments, and to contribute to their families and communities financially. To foster these benefits, programs were developed to support people in having meaningful work. For the more entrepreneurially inclined, micro-loans offered support to start small businesses. For those who worked well with a structure, a salary-splitting program encouraged existing companies to hire employees with addictions. (Unfortunately, these programs were most vulnerable to budget cuts.)

By 2016, the number of people addicted to heroin in Portugal was down from one hundred thousand people to twenty-five thousand, and Portugal had the lowest overdose mortality rate in Western Europe. The integrated approach of medical professionals, law enforcement, social services, and job enhancement programs were significant to this success.

This is a vastly different trend for addicts than the one underway in North America with its linear "war on drugs" approach. Nearly as many people died from overdoses in 2016 in the US (approximately sixty-four thousand) as died in the Vietnam, Afghanistan, and Iraq wars combined.

Shifting the Portuguese action plan on addiction from controlling criminal behaviour to generating feelings of belonging among good neighbors created many side benefits. Through this circular thinking plan to step into the unknown, the implementers discovered that employment went up, while healthcare and law enforcement costs went down significantly. At the same time, the improved sense of community, reduced individual and family suffering, and the benefit of the healthier lifestyles of Portuguese citizens was priceless. Furthermore, a new global understanding of good governance was introduced to the world, which is a gift that keeps on giving.

Circular thinking has optimal times for implementation such as when you want to create connections. As a consultant to a First Nation, I recall a time when I benefitted from a lesson in when to have a circular mindset. During preparations for a workshop aimed at getting feedback on programming, we considered ways to enlist participants. It was proposed that we provide lunch and snacks, gas money, per diems, daycare, and an impressive array of draw prizes, all to encourage people to join us.

The last one triggered me to say, "Isn't this getting a bit crazy? People should come because they are concerned about the topic of the meeting. If they don't come, that's good information. They are saying they have no concerns about these programs." I was pushing back against possible distractions from the topic and high expenditures.

Lawrence Joe, my nephew by marriage, said, "No, it's not crazy. You are talking as a privileged white person."

Family can be so disarmingly direct. I'm quite proud of myself here. Years ago, I would have clammed up or suggested he had misunderstood me. But I honestly thought I had a good point. I was curious about how he saw it differently. I asked, "Can you explain that to me?"

"Sure," I recall him saying. "You're imagining that the only purpose of the meeting is to deliver our information. (He was right.) That is one intention of the meeting, but there are several others. If someone comes for the prizes and they participate, we have an opportunity to hear from someone we normally wouldn't. We want that range of opinions. Diverse opinions help us make better decisions. If that person just listens, later, when he is out with his friends, he might talk about what he heard to a person we don't normally reach. That's a welcome bonus for us because we want our program information to reach as many people as possible. If someone comes just to be social, it builds their sense of being part of our community. Generating that sense of belonging among our citizens is more important to us than delivering information, in the big picture. And if someone is there because they need the money or the food, it is good that we have this opportunity to pay our people and give them respect for contributing their valuable knowledge. We want to take care of our people. This meeting is not just about getting feedback on our program initiatives."

I realized Lawrence was going out on a limb for me when he took the time to explain the nature of the clash between our thinking styles, and that it must be exhausting to repeatedly do this for people in linear thinking mode. When he explained it to me, I could see the wisdom of his way. I was thinking in terms of people being interested or not interested in our information, and on-track or off-track with the agenda. Lawrence was seeing a variety of possible benefits, all leading to greater connections.

I made a mental note to pause and really absorb what is being offered when an Indigenous person teaches me something that is counter to my current way of thinking. While it is not Indigenous people's job to teach circular thinking, it has occasionally been their gift to me. By paying close attention, I am offering gratitude in return. By telling the story to others, I hope I am paying it forward.

My pitfall was failing to recognize two distinct modes of thinking. In linear mode, there is a tendency to assume everyone thinks linearly. This is one of the features of linear thinking that we will explore more in Chapter 5. When in this mindset, and things start to go badly, it is easiest to assume that the other person just isn't very good at playing the game.

The challenge in this situation, as in business, cross-cultural relationships, governance, and in our personal lives, is to disengage from our current mindset by "going to the bridge" to better see the other option.

Wisdom leaders have tried to prepare us for this insight for centuries. Elder Albert Marshall of the Eskasoni Mi'kmaq First Nation on Cape Breton Island framed the challenge of today as the need to practice "two-eyed seeing." He described us as living in a time for "learning to see from one eye with the strengths of Indigenous knowledges and ways of knowing, and from the other eye with the strengths of Western knowledges and ways of knowing...and learning to use both these eyes together, for the benefit of all." This is good advice for everyone. Dogrib Chief Jimmy Bruneau advised his people in 1971 that they need to be "strong like two people." The Tłı̨chǫ School Board (one of the first Aboriginal-run school boards in Canada) adopted this philosophy, understanding it to mean "we must embrace our culture and the associated values rooted in that history, as well as the Western way. It is important for achieving success in today's world." The Irish poet W. B. Yeats provocatively hinted at the presence of these two choices all around us when he said, "There is another world, and it is in this one." From many sources, we are hearing of the value of understanding these two ways of knowing.

In Ury's negotiation, and my community meeting preparations, the parties began in different frames of mind. When we know there are two states of mind to choose from, we can pause to read the situation and become open to the possibility that we are in an unproductive or incompatible state of mind. This realization creates the potential for crossing the distance between the parties.

Scientific research has also been revealing that we have two foundational mindsets. I was encouraged when I read neuro-anatomist Jill Bolte Taylor's book, *My Stroke of Insight*.

One day, during a massive stroke, Taylor experienced her consciousness shifting between what she describes as her left and
right brain. Luckily for everyone, she lived to tell the story.
Hearing a neuroscientist describe these two radically different states of mind from first-hand experience is illuminating,
in part because she had the observational language to convey
them.

With vivid descriptions, Taylor shares her shift from one
way of knowing to the other. At first, she cared deeply about
the present moment. She felt connected to her body and the
energy in everything around her. This flooded her with feelings of "curiosity and love." The world made sense because,
"in this moment, we are perfect. We are whole. And we are
beautiful." Taylor was happy and fascinated with the experience of this mindset. She just wanted to stay where she was
in this moment (what I would refer to as the experience of
circular thinking).

Then perception sharply shifted in her brain. Taylor became
very focused on finding details and more details to categorize
and organize, in a drive to increase the predictability of her
environment. She wanted to take what she knew about the
past and use it to navigate towards a safer future. She felt separate from the external world, like it was there for her to use,
and objectively driven to control her environment to achieve
her goals. (This is a good description of a linear mindset.)

This linear thinking mode turned out to have been life-
saving because, at that point, she had precious few moments
to figure out how to use a phone to get help before she died.
Fortunately, she achieved her goal and called for help.

The amazing thing about Taylor's experience is that the
stroke created a clear separation of what she calls her left and
right brain thinking. Experiencing this separation gave her
profound insights into her years of study. In other words,
it became clear that two ways of knowing are part of the

construction of being human. They are distinct, and we are biologically designed to shift from one to the other. It suggests we can't be in both mindsets at the same time, although we can fluctuate from one to the other quite rapidly.

Recent scientific studies on how the mind works have also concluded that this dual nature is fundamental to the human condition. They have been variously called attachment and survival mode; Type A and Type B personalities, masculine and feminine dynamics (not to be confused with male and female), "flight or fight" versus "tend and befriend" behaviours, and passion and pain drivers.

I suggest these are all references to the same two mindsets. I like to call them linear and circular thinking.

The first time I spoke publicly on what was to become known as the 2 Ways of Knowing (2WK) Project was at the 2012 Yukon Geoscience Forum in Whitehorse. There was a modest audience of geologists and First Nation members in the room. I was apprehensive because chances were pretty good that someone would feel challenged by my simple summary of thinking styles. The model assumes that individual and collective thought is part of a larger pattern. Some take this as a challenge to their independent thought processes. Worst of all, I dreaded the possibility that no one would connect to my theory and instead find me boring.

I decided to go back to the mindset I had adopted when interviewing for my land claims negotiator position. I just had to speak from my heart. I believed I was seeing a meaningful pattern and I was interested in other people's thoughts. To my delight, I received two inspiring pieces of feedback from my talk. A First Nation woman approached me after the talk and said, "You have found a way to explain it to them! Thank you." Later, as I sat in another talk, Michael Roper of Agnico Eagle turned around in his chair from the row in front of me, gave me his card, and looking over the top of his glasses, said, "I was at your talk yesterday. It was a good talk. I've never heard First Nation engagement explained that way before." Then he added, with a playful glint in his eye, "Also possibly the best therapy I've ever had." This made me laugh. I understood him to be saying that he almost effortlessly popped out of his worldview and got a glimpse of another perspective. It was an "aha" moment. I also wondered if he might be right — how much of relationship therapy is the struggle to transport ourselves from our default thinking mode to that of our partner?

Protect the Differences

The differences between linear and circular thinking are what make them powerful. We need to protect their distinct properties if we want to access the best each has to offer.

Terri L. Kelly is the former CEO of W. L. Gore & Associates, one of the most successful innovation companies in the world. She was surprised when her peers nominated her as their new CEO (or, in Gore & Associates terms, 'unCEO'). Gore & Associates has a unique culture that seeks out and elevates people who understand natural (circular) leadership. They want people who are highly motivated, with a strong internal compass, and fearless when it comes to asking questions. Leaders emerge when a significant number of associates choose to follow them. In this situation, if someone calls a meeting, participants are responsible for determining if the meeting will be a good use of their time and responding authentically. As a result, leaders must have insightful and respectful relationships with their co-workers in order to attract their participation.

When hiring a new CEO, Gore & Associates asks a broad spectrum of their 9,000 employees whom they would like to follow. Kelly's surprise probably says a lot about why she was chosen.

Rather than pursuing a linear track to the top of a hierarchy, circular thinkers focus on bringing their best self to the job and working well with people in support of their ability to do the same.

Kelly described her company as having two kinds of people. In a *Fast Company* interview she said, "We have what we call rainmakers and implementers. Rainmakers come up with wild ideas, implementers make them real. The two drive each other crazy. If you're not careful, control will gravitate to the implementers. So, we protect the rainmakers. This means we have to be comfortable with more chaos." Kelly says she spends most of her time emphasizing difference and preventing people from reverting to conventional wisdom.

Note that the moment they were named, the two very distinct roles came into conscious existence in the organization. From then on, the unique operating requirements of each role could be seen and supported. Gore & Associates has made protecting the differences between what I would call their linear and circular thinkers a fundamental part of their organizational structure and it has resulted in innovation success.

Kelly saw her leadership role as having the insight to recognize the two types of employees the company depended on, and understanding the operating principles that support their distinct gifts. In the face of chaos, we are not always best served by re-establishing our comfort zone of predictability and order. Instead, we can say, "Yes, I am uncomfortable, and I am also curious." Following the curiosity leads to the magic. Meanwhile, linear thinkers can be tasked with keeping the rainmakers safe from external dangers. In this way, leaders capitalize on the optimal use of both mindsets.

I had an experience that is embarrassing in hindsight but was also profound to me. It was my first recognition of the intense feeling of immersion in a linear mindset.

It was in the early days of developing the 2WK theory

when a colleague requested that we meet to discuss the model. My first reaction was hesitation. I worried that the theory was not ready, but I controlled my fear of failure and accepted the meeting. I was determined to put together an outstanding presentation on the principles of the bridge. I even designed an original explanatory diagram that was particularly helpful. Armed with the tools to overcome any obstacle, I headed out the door.

We met at his place, to facilitate parking, and, after a drink, walked to a nearby restaurant. As I stepped into the restaurant, my confidence in being able to effectively explain the framework dipped. It would be difficult, maybe even impossible, to share my explanatory diagram with such poor lighting and small tables.

Things just slid downhill from there.

Every time I left space for him to contribute a reflection on the model, he carried the conversation off on a tangent. Either he did not get the concept, which spurred my efforts, or he had limited ability to focus!

When we got back to his place, he asked me in for another drink, (this guy was big on hydration) and I thought, "I can draw my explanatory diagram in there!"

We sat side by side on the couch as I, at last, had a visual aid. When he leaned forward, I thought, "Now he's interested!"

It was only then that I realized the obvious: I was at a meeting and he was on a date.

It seems so clear in retrospect, even to me. However, in that moment, I only saw the need to explain the model in a way that informed and convinced. I either ignored information pointing to an alternative dimension or used it to confirm my biases.

It was such a valuable lesson. Linear focus on a goal can be so hypnotizing that it convinces us that we are right in our thinking. My only measure of success was the amount of progress I made on my action plan. It was nearly impossible to break free of the intoxicating drive of linear thinking and see the other dimensions of this event.

The bridge understanding of linear and circular thinking makes possible the kind of insightful disengagement I needed that evening. It prompts us to acknowledge the operating principles we are employing. Again, it is like Ury's "going to the balcony." The difference is that when we "go to the bridge" we can apply the two sets of operating principles we'll consider in Chapter 5, and evaluate the options.

On that evening I could have thought, "I am focused on my plan to deliver information. That's linear. What is driving him? Ah. He was clearly exploring a variety of directions in order to make a personal connection. That's circular. No wonder this feels awkward. And with these questions I am already on the bridge.

This is a big point, so I will offer another story about the stark differences between the two ways of knowing and how using the bridge helps to see them. The first time I saw Allison Rippin-Armstrong, Kaminak Gold Corporation's vice president of sustainability, she was giving a talk on First Nation engagement at the 2014 Yukon Geoscience Forum. Rippin-Armstrong has an excellent track record of meaningful engagement with local communities. She offered this analogy for the way many companies go astray when they approach First Nation communities.

> When I first met my husband of now over twenty-five years, if I had said, "Let's have three children, four dogs, and six horses, and let's live on acreage way out in the country. Also, you should know, my work will probably have me away a lot, and for more than a few years we will really struggle financially."
> If I had introduced myself with that statement as we

sat at our first dinner, that young man would have made a run for it. And who would have blamed him?

Why would we think it is any different when, as a mining company, we meet with a First Nation? It is just like dating. Starting with a description of the project outcome is no way to start a relationship. We have to start with conversations, one person at a time, to find out what is important to each of us. We need to know where we have common interests. This is the place where we can start to trust each other.

The big message I got here was that we can't use the same attitude that we use to engineer a mine to meaningfully engage with communities and Indigenous governments. Circular thinking is focused on relationships and building trust, while linear thinking is focused on goals and progress. Today, it is becoming clear that we need capacity for both ways of thinking, to cover all aspects of a project.

At the Prospectors and Developers Association of Canada 2016 conference, Brent Bergeron, then Goldcorp's executive vice president of executive affairs and sustainability, shared a similar message to a packed audience. He talked about his experience as part of the negotiation team that concluded the highly respected collaboration agreement (also known as an impact benefit agreement or IBA) between the Cree Nation of Wemindji and Goldcorp, regarding the Éléonore gold mine project in Quebec. He said that he is often asked if the agreement meets the UN standard of "free, prior, and informed consent."

He said he responds by saying,

I don't know. I don't even care. I think the principle of free, prior, and informed consent is important, but I will not go into a community thinking I have to tick off that box. What builds a mine is relationships. It is an ongoing commitment to being open and transparent – like a marriage. We want [the relationship] to be so strong that it can withstand the hard times – and we do have them.

Bergeron went on to acknowledge that seeking this kind of connection with local communities is a more vulnerable position for the company to place themselves in than focusing on meeting regulatory requirements, but it also has many advantages.

Asking for a recipe to meet a standard is an expedient way to overcome a regulatory obstacle. The questioner wants to codify and therefore limit the requirements for free, prior, and informed consent – a list of boxes to check off. "We've done a, b, and c and therefore, the standard has been met" (whether or not the other party feels heard or is supportive).

Contrast this with a circular negotiation, where the parties meet to understand each other and find overlap between their diverse perspectives. The outcome is customized to the unique relationship between the parties. In this model, the parties may decide on a mutual description of what satisfied free, prior, and informed consent, or make a statement of principle and revisit the meaning of it in a year, or every five years until the end of the project because they value keeping the agreement relevant and making their relationships more resilient over time.

Bergeron, Rippin-Armstrong, and I (eventually) all recognized the same mismatch between the two frames of mind. A linear mindset is about pushing back against obstacles, inefficient use of time, and inconsistency. When variables are predictable, we can count on this linear mindset to keep us productive and successful. A circular mindset customizes to individual project needs, and develops trust by engaging in a responsive discussion, now and into the future. In times of great change, when we need to work well together, and have reached the limits of our normal ways of operating, circular thinking is our best option.

At least since the Industrial Revolution, dominant societies have privileged linear over circular thinking. Today, rather than seeing a competition between the mindsets, the idea of recognizing and protecting both mindsets is taking hold. The first step towards having two ways of knowing respected within a project is to consciously separate them and protect their differences.

Separate But Together

Linear thinkers fear that the second they let their guard down, there is a hole in the safety net. This attitude maintains an important and effective defense against danger. The problem is, this mentality also keeps the door to circular thinking shut – unless we figure out a way to allow the two contrasting realities to co-exist.

A Northern Tutchone First Nation Elder explained to me the principle of remaining separate but together. Holding his arms parallel in front of him, his hands clenched in fists, he said, "You have to know who you are, and you have to let them be strong by being who they are. Don't mix them. Then you can work beside each other, and benefit from each other." He interwove his fingers and then pointed his index fingers forward. "Some days you can find a way to connect your way and their way. You have to keep separate and then find a way to work together. This is when you have something good."

Linear thinking builds groups with high productivity, accountability, justice, safety, and excellence; it secures personal comforts and predictability. When circular thinking permeates a culture, there is a sense of belonging and an ability to be authentic. This fosters many things including creative problem solving, transformational cultures, and personal happiness.

Imagine sitting down to paint a picture with a dish of white and a dish of black paint. If you mixed the two together before painting, all you have to work with is grey. If you use them separately you can create contrasting patterns.

When linear and circular thinking are each recognized by their internal order, it becomes clear that they are functional opposites of each other. Distinct but together, they can be mutually supportive of the creation of a successful project.

Dick Whittington, CEO of Farallon Mining, created a unique organizational structure for the G-9 Mine in Guerrero State, Mexico. Whittington designated two positions that reported directly to him, the general manager of mines and the general manager of social economics. Each was given the power to shut down the mine without first calling Whittington.

"I did this because I looked at the personalities involved. The GM of the mine was an alpha male – wants things done now, get out of my way, no excuses," Whittington explained. "I estimated that these qualities made him good at achieving production. The GM of social economics was highly empathetic. I had a lot of people in the social economics department, twenty-five or so, because I wanted to send a big message to the local community that this was important to me."

The GM of mines was located at the mine site, which was all about gates, security systems, and aspects of tonnage and grade. The social economics office was in the exploration camp, totally removed from the mine, and had a comfortable seating area. The social economics workers' jobs were to know the people of the community and get a sense of the conversations around the dinner tables.

"I wanted people in a Farallon safety jacket in the

community every day. God gave us two eyes, two ears, and one mouth for a reason. I wanted people to know us and be relaxed around us," said Whittington.

One day, the GM of social economics walked into the mine office and gave the order to shut down production. The GM of mines picked up the phone and made it happen. Then he must have asked, "Why!?" The GM of social economics recognized a simmering dissatisfaction among the locals that was building a negative attitude toward the mine. They needed to figure out what the problem was.

When Whittington got the call back in Vancouver, he said, "Good. This will give us a chance to show the community our values."

He said, "We stopped revenue for thirty days while we talked to the local women and men. We learned that our trucks were driving down the road, dusty as hell, spreading red dust all over their laundry as it hung on the line. These are poor people, and very proud. The women do laundry every day to show that their families are well cared for and the men take pride in their appearance."

This issue is an excellent example of something that is meaningful in the circular world but of low priority in the linear world of cost and productivity data. Can you imagine going to the GM of mines to explain the seriousness of your laundry issue? The G-9 Mine was organized to make room for doing exactly that. They included both ways of assessing what is important.

Once value was given to the community's feelings, trust began and the resolution wasn't rocket science.

"In the end, we agreed to send the trucks in a convoy at 7 a.m., when the dew was highest. Water trucks drove at the front and at the end of the ore truck convoy. We completely stopped trucking while the laundry was drying, and ladies were at the market," Whittington reported.

But the real point was that the company showed they would listen, openly share their perspective, and work with the community to jointly solve problems. When future issues arose, the community rapidly came forward to explain their views, making it easier to understand and address the heart of the issue. The community respected the company enough to raise issues that concerned them in a timely and constructive manner.

Paying attention to both linear and circular aspects of mining during that first crisis resulted in a stable workforce which saved significant operational expenses.

"People didn't want to leave their jobs at G-9, and the community was happy to have us there; actively supported us," Whittington said with pride. "This is our competitive advantage."

Today, organizational structures, conflict resolution negotiations, and environmental movements are intuitively developing their circular thinking. As Terri Kelly of Gore & Associates, and Dick Whittington of Farallon Mining found, and the Northern Tutchone elder advised, this often requires consciously valuing and protecting circular operating principles from linear thinking. When linear structures work in concert with circular principles, a new competitive advantage is achieved.

Chapter 2
I've Got a Name

Naming is the powerful act of causing something to come into conscious existence. When it came to naming the two modes of thinking in *The Bridge*, I asked myself what was most important for the name to convey. I realized the best word would capture the experience of each thinking mode. The term "linear thinking" was instantly recognized and accepted by all the people I polled as a common way of thinking. "Circular thinking" was another matter. "Why would anyone want to go around in circles?" was a common response.

Finding language without baggage for the second way of thinking was hard. I had felt that frustration of hopelessly returning to the same place when I'm trying to make progress, so I searched for a better word.

Then I realized that what they really meant was that nobody who is in linear thinking mode wants to be in a *Groundhog Day* kind of loop. But, as the movie demonstrates, when focusing on making progress becomes impossible, we are freed from the need to make progress. With this realization, returning to the same situation becomes a welcome opportunity to discover what is truly meaningful.

I also realized that choosing a term that people actively avoid is counter-productive, no matter how accurate it is. (I know this because I named my first book *The Virgin's Promise*.

If I had a clean kitchen for each time I have explained that the word "virgin" means to know you are of value just for being yourself, like a virgin forest, I would be blissful.)

At the same time, using a term more socially acceptable could negate what is new in this idea. Its full potential might fail to be brought to life. This happened to neuroscientist Marian Diamond in the 1960s when female scientists struggled to be taken seriously. She chose a socially acceptable descriptor for her findings on childhood development, and produced unexpected consequences.

Diamond did landmark research on play and brain development. She discovered that rats raised in an environment with a variety of fun toys, free time, and playfully loving relationships grew up to be smarter, with larger and more complex brains. Loathe to use words like "playful," "fun," and "toys" – afraid of being judged frivolous, as most female scientists were in the sixties – Diamond described this environment as "enriched."

What parent doesn't want their kid to be smarter, with a big, complex brain? Leagues of North American parents in the 80s and 90s set out to "enrich" the nursery with stimulating mobiles and colourful murals. However, what the research had shown was that babies benefit from playing with a favourite toy, and from a parent's smile and tickles. Babies probably felt so confused as they lay alone in their cribs, their view-scape populated with black and white mobiles, as a Baby Einstein tape droned in the background.

I have gained enormous respect for the power of word choice by embarking on this project. Carefully using language that distinguishes linear and circular operating principles makes them available to our conscious thought processes. It's like gaining a bridge to walk between two distinct landscapes.

At the Global Exploration, Mining and Minerals

(GEMM2020) gathering on solutions for responsible mining, I found myself a seat and introduced myself to the man beside me. When he asked about my work, I gave my elevator pitch for circular and linear thinking.

He smiled from ear to ear and said, "I have a story for you. My boss told it to me, and we use it as a guiding principle almost every day."

Each time I recall this story I'm grateful for how elegantly it keeps offering me insights. Here's what I remember of what he said.

In the 1970s, at a public meeting in a predominantly Indigenous northern Alberta community, an oil and gas company geologist stood at the front of the room. Basically, he was delivering information like "Here's where we'll be going," and "Here's what we'll be doing."

The locals sat in silent rows, watching the presentation. When the geologist finished talking, a First Nation Elder walked to the front and drew a line on the chalkboard.

"This is the most dangerous thing the white man has brought us," he said.

Silence. The geologist must have felt a pang of concern, wondering where this was going.

Then the elder drew a big circle on the board.

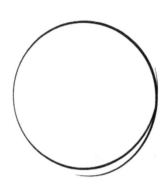

"This is the way we see things."
He paused, waiting for everyone to think about that.
Then he drew more circles.

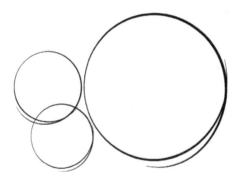

"See. You can't cover all the ground without overlapping the circles," he explained. "In our way, no matter what, you always want to connect with each other. You're better off when you share, reach towards each other, and respect what other people are saying. Otherwise, someone, or something, important gets left out."

Then he drew boxes abutting that original line.

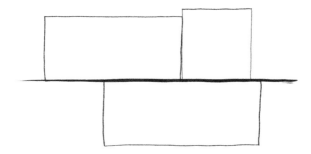

"With lines, you can cover all the ground. No need to over-lap. Now I can say, 'This is mine,'" he said, pointing to one of the boxes, "'and that is yours,'" pointing at the other.

Then he added, "Now we just have to fight over where that line goes."

With provocative clarity, the Elder showed the two mind-sets for facing the world, and how fundamentally different they are.

I decided the term "circular thinking" is the right term for the second way of thinking because it opened several doors to good discussions. It will be difficult for linear thinkers to see its value in the beginning, and I take on the challenge of making that value clear in the pages of this book.

In the meantime, if "circular thinking" sounds like the opposite of a good idea, see it as a sign that you are in linear thinking mode, where progress is king. The question becomes, how do I step into circular thinking mode for a while? What would the opposite of trying to make progress look like? It involves returning to the same place on a deeper level in the search for meaning.

One of many "aha" moments from writing this book is the realization that the struggle to shift from linear to circular thinking parallels the challenge of de-colonization. Colonization and property ownership are concepts grounded in linear thinking. Leaving colonial behaviours behind requires the ability to practice circular thinking. This effort to transform requires a conceptualization of two different ways of knowing in modern life. Too often I see the same concept with the players taking different positions. Linear thinking can only preserve and protect what already exists. It needs to be suspended while we learn to become experts in circular thinking and incorporate it into our systems. Then there hope for some societal transformation.

Examples of how linear thinking drives management principles, education, business, and medical practices are easy to find. However, the language for circular thinking is less recognizable in Western society. This is problematic because it means that part of our thinking potential is less available. Opportunities for circular thinking are all around us, but they are invisible until they are named.

The big challenge I accepted in writing this book is to find language that separates and activates linear and circular thinking. The northern Albertan Elder's story directed me to the insight that each thinking mode has a unique set of operating principles. The language choice for linear and circular thinking has to highlight the ways they are opposite in their operating nature.

Linear thinking is driven by concepts like compartmentalization, comparison, excellence, goal achievement, efficiency, paramountcy, safety, and consistency: things that are evidenced in the physical world. The more resources and motivation an individual and their allies have, the more competitive advantages they have for expanding the size of their box. In this world, a finite amount of property is to be divided among the players.

Circular thinking cares about things like sharing, respect,

inclusion, resilience, engagement, transformation, imagination, belonging, and authenticity. These are internal states of being. The sizes of each of the circles are a representation of a person's self-awareness, their ability to listen to others, and their capacity to grow and make connections. The area of overlap of the circles is where group wisdom is found. The more overlap, the more collective power there is in the system. There is no limit to how big the circles can get.

The following chart provides language for the respective benefits and qualities of linear and circular thinking. It is by no means exhaustive.

LINEAR THINKING	CIRCULAR THINKING
Efficiency	Effectiveness
Loyalty	Authenticity, caring
Control, endurance	Freedom, resilience
Winning, comparison, competition	Engaging, collaboration, cooperation
Excellence	Creativity
Motivation by negative consequences	Inspiration by inner guidance system
Justice, law and order, regulations, rules	Reconciliation, belonging, healing
Predictability, certainty	Novelty, transformation, change
Fairness	Customization
Project management	Natural leadership
Progress	Play
Skills, practice	Talents, purpose
Logic	Intuition, gut feeling, heart
Direction, goals	Meaning, insights, principles
Comfort and safety	Happiness and joy
Membership	Belonging

Everyone is capable of linear and circular thinking. The bridge helps us recognize our dominant ability and hone it; we can also recognize the different abilities of others and appreciate, delegate to, and support them; and we can expand our capacity in our lower-comfort thinking style. It all begins by seeing two distinct ways of thinking as parts of our whole thinking ability.

Failing to recognize the distinctness of linear and circular thinking, often results in one word that carries two meanings. At some point in a conversation, people are not on the same side of the bridge and a circus of miscommunication ensues. It's a "Who's on first?" kind of Abbott and Costello routine. And sometimes it is not so funny. Here are words that carry two meanings. Imagine how easily conversations could derail when people are using different definitions of the same word.

	LINEAR DEFINITION	CIRCULAR DEFINITION
Problem	The need to overcome an obstacle and shape my desired outcome	A call to read the meaning behind a situation and support personal reconnection
Negotiation	Transactional contract with concretizing terms	Reciprocal arrangements with living terms
Membership	A place of compliance-based, conditional acceptance	A place of belonging
Transparency	Saying what I am going to do, doing it, and reporting back when it is done; strategic	Making information of interest to you available in the format you prefer; inclusive
Relationships	Allies who share a goal	Friends who care about each other
Truth	The provable or measurable facts	An authentic personal perspective

	LINEAR DEFINITION	CIRCULAR DEFINITION
Sustainability	Designed for longevity, achieved through design; the preservation and protection of existing work	The ability to create ongoing and generative spin-off benefits
Well-being	Comfort and safety	Happiness and connection
Success	Being productive; achieving goals	Being authentic; awakening to meaning
Vulnerability	Exposure to danger	Being open-hearted, receptive
Respect	Recognition for achievements, skills, position, and contributions	Recognition of the intrinsic worth in every being
Listening	Filtering to identify obstacles, and to get agreement or strategic information	Making an effort to understand and connect with the speaker
Honesty	Not telling a lie	Giving a genuine feeling, free of manipulation
Growth	Obtaining a larger piece of the pie	Expanding one's consciousness
Good	Aligned with acceptable practices	A feeling of alignment with who you know yourself to be
Care	Caution	Open-heartedness
Justice	Retributive	Retorative

I met Kenny, a First Nation member, at a pitch session.

He said, "Okay, you've got this tool to help us engage. Then explain to me why [mineral companies] keep lying to us."

"Can you give me an example?" I asked with curiosity.

"Sure. They meet with us, and they tell us one thing. Then we meet them later and they tell us another important thing, that they must have known before but never told us."

I knew right away where the disconnection was coming from. The companies and Kenny had different understandings of transparency.

"I'm guessing that you think that the people you are engaging with are working to know what you care about and to give you any relevant information that will support that." (I see this as finding areas of overlap.) "They would openly share information because they recognize that when we share openly, we have access to more creative and robust ideas. It is also the best way to develop trust."

Kenny nodded.

"The companies see transparency differently," I said. "They are being strategic about moving the process forward. They want to offer only the information that will lead to making progress towards their goal. Anything else might cause the process to lose focus. They will include anything you directly ask for, and won't fabricate information, but they won't add things that might complicate the talks. Transparency to them means saying what they're going to do, doing it, and reporting back when it is done. It is narrowly focused on their goal and centred on physical action."

This kind of disconnect is common when circular and linear thinkers meet with different understandings of the meaning of the same word.

Other times, a linear word is used to describe a circular process. Like two people both trying to push from opposite sides on a two-man crosscut wood saw, it is very frustrating.

When several Yukon First Nation Land Claim Agreements were completed, these First Nations found themselves facing the daunting task of developing new governments. The department names were probably chosen in the interest of being consistent with existing government structures (consistency being a linear value). It made sense at the time because the linear regimes were up and running, with decades of experience and fine tuning behind them. Also, the parties had to be able to work together. Without a modern model for the operating principles circular thinking, it was hard to pause to explore new potentials and create systems that support two different worldviews operating together. This is how linear words became part of Yukon First Nations' governments.

One day, while working on his master's thesis on the Peel Watershed Regional Land Use Plan, Colin O'Neil walked into a room where Yukon First Nation members and employees were talking about the word "resources." He heard this conversation:

There's got to be a better word than 'resources'. I mean, it doesn't fit with the First Nations' perspective at all.

Yeah, it's very government. Something we will manage and control.

As a word, it completely erases the connections that people have with so-called 'resources.' Saying the caribou is a 'resource'? It's the same way that forestry companies treat the trees. Everything is so compartmentalized.

It's the same way that corporations treat their employees.

Yeah. But here we are, talking about 'resources.' We have a Natural 'Resources' Department; we're going to the table with the Yukon Government to talk about 'resources.' It doesn't fit with the way this government thinks at all.

What would the alternative be?

Umm...I don't know. I guess there isn't one, because the whole idea of 'resources' is grounded in a way of thinking about that thing. It's separating it from yourself, from its connections and relations. Like how the elders are always talking about everything being connected. You can't think that way and also think in terms of 'resources.'

What would the alternative be? It is a good question. Resources refers to objects that are separate from us and available for our use. It is a linear perspective. What would be a circular counterpart? Something that describes the intention to be in good connection with all forms of nature as we do our activities. How about the Department of Being Respect? (Being referring to all forms of nature as well what we embody.) Not ideal, but it helps us imagine how different the work of that department would be.

With experience, Indigenous governments have been able to assess the suitability, or lack of suitability, of linear principles for their wildlife stewardship programs. Indigenous scholars such as Robin Wall Kimmerer are also making great strides in what circular wildlife "management" would look like through principles such as reciprocity.

In other cases, Indigenous peoples have added a chair at their wildlife stewardship meetings for every being with an interest in the topic of discussion. For non-human entities, like water and caribou, someone sits in those chairs and speaks from the perspective of the water or the caribou. Imagine that.

Being mindful of the language we use ensures we are effectively communicating in circular or linear ways. Hari Tulsidas, the economic affairs officer of the Sustainable Energy Division of the UN Economic Commission for Europe shared some of his ideas on effective community engagement at a meeting including developing governments and mining companies.

Tulsidas encouraged the mining community to change the names they use to describe themselves.

My interest was piqued.

Tulsidas suggested that terms such as extractive industry, mineral extraction, commodities, mineral exploitation, and resource value chain are all highly objective, de-humanizing, and production-focused terms. They come off as aggressive and fear-inducing to people outside the industry.

He had a point. The word "extraction" reminds me of being in the dentist's chair. It sounds like a nightmare in which the dentist isn't aware that the tooth decay he's attacking is attached to a human being – namely me!

The process of mining also feels much more personal to the nearby community than the word "extraction" suggests.

Evidently, Lightstorm Entertainment and 20th Century Fox thought so, too, when they made a mining company the villain of their blockbuster movie *Avatar*. The studios felt it was credible to characterize a mineral company as a ruthless exploiter of the environment with no compassion for the local inhabitants. *Avatar* made $2.4 billion at the box office world-wide, one of the highest-grossing movies of all time, which means there is a pretty good chance that when companies describe themselves as the extractive industry, local communities envision bulldozers rolling over "Mother Tree" and local inhabitants to get to the "unobtainium" below.

Impressed by this emphasis on the importance of word choice, I started noticing the language used when addressing other issues. It is declared that "cancer can be beaten" as if dropping the gauntlet against an external enemy. What if the slogan was, "Let's understand your cancer"? Focus would be placed on the development of personalized treatments and the impact cancer has on individuals' lives.

Jeffrey Rediger has an interesting career as medical director for the McLean SouthEast Adult Psychiatric Programs and an assistant professor of psychiatry at Harvard Medical School. He also followed his interest in theology including a Master of Divinity degree from Princeton's Theological Seminary. His work is done at the controversial intersection of medicine, psychiatry and spirituality. In his book *Cured: Strengthen Your Immune System and Heal Your Life,* Rediger rigorously explores cases of spontaneous healing of incurable diseases looking for a pattern. His studies only included cases of diseases defined as incurable, with medically indisputable evidence of accurate diagnosis, clear physical evidence of recovery, and no complicating factors. He then looked as this subset of cases to discover a pattern.

Rediger concluded that there are four gems in the black box of medical miracles. They include changing your nutrition in a loving way to reduce inflammation, supporting your immune system, eliminating chronic stress in your life, and exploring your identity including repairing false beliefs.

I noticed all these factors relate to individuals. The last component is literally circular power (as we will see in Chapter 4).

The words we use to frame an issue shape the answers that we find. Unfortunate word choices can send a program off on the wrong track. For example, Peter Cohen, in his paper "The Naked Empress: Modern Neuroscience and the Concept of Addiction," suggests that the word "addict" is wrong. If the name is lacking in rigour, any treatment or remedy that follows will be insufficient. Cohen also declares that he doesn't know any scientists who are interested in addicts. They are interested in the brain. This means their research mostly involves spending time with rats and mice which will dislocate their research from people.

I think he has a point. If addiction is related to a personal sense of engagement in life, as the Rat Park experiment suggests, the nature of being human needs to be part of the answer. The word "addict" sets up a "them and us" mentality where addicts are seen as a threat to society that needs to be controlled through laws and consequences. Non-addicts are seen as good citizens worthy of protection. Alternatively, when addiction is described as a disease, our focus shifts to battling a medical issue that is unrelated to social issues. This is a profound difference brought about by our word choice.

Cohen believes addiction should be characterized as a crisis of bonding. He sees the decision to use drugs as a human response to distressed feelings of disconnection from one's personal worth, and consequently the ability to have friends, and a sense of belonging in the bigger community.

When the issue is recognized as a lack of bonding, the societal response is focused on restoring a shared sense of belonging. Efforts are made to increase social cohesion and support individuals with a caring attitude. Whether addiction is described as a danger to society, a medical issue, or a crisis of bonding has a huge impact on the type of action we take in response to the issue.

My favourite outcome of careful use of language is that it creates access to linear and circular worlds. Our spoken, written, and body languages express either linear or circular thinking and move us into one of those two worlds.

Chapter 3
Why Only Two?

"Why only two?"

I hear this question a lot, along with variations on the statement, "There are infinite ways of knowing." It is true. Each culture, country, business, and person develops a unique way of navigating life and making meaning.

Yet, in the bigger picture, the one seen when we step way back from the details, there is a grand pattern within all this uniqueness. There are repeated examples of opposite pairs of words needed to cover all sides of an idea. Pain and pleasure, survive and flourish, compete and collaborate, meaning and direction, to name a few. Even the answer to this question of why only two comes from two sources: the circular experience and the linear research.

The Experiential Perspective

From my circular perspective, I know there are two ways of knowing because that is what I experience. I muse that perhaps we have circular and linear thinking modes because two is the minimum number of states required to create a pattern. For example, computer programing depends on the contrast of zeros and ones to create an infinite variety of products.

In circular thinking mode, this personal observation is valid, even without scientific study, logic, or expert advice.

A stark contrast between circular and linear thinking was presented to me in the summer of 1987 when I accepted a contract working for First Nation clients.

After graduating with an applied master's in mineral exploration, I spent my last $1700 on a truck and headed to the Klondike goldfields in the Yukon. I intended to prospect for the mother lode. When I wasn't wandering the hills hammering on rocks, I spent my evenings at Diamond Tooth Gerties' gambling hall. On one of these nights, the Yukon land claim negotiation teams were in town and several First Nation men asked to join my table. Normally I didn't talk geology unless I was looking for a mass exodus, but they seemed genuinely interested. Next thing I knew, they were saying things like, "You seem to really know geology," and "Would you like to do an evaluation of our lands for us?"

Would I!? Evaluating mineral potential was my dream job. I said yes on the spot.

I received many protective warnings and more than a few cold shoulders from the geology community during the months of research that followed; I found myself standing on the "wrong" side of the line between "them" and "us." I was surprised. In my mind, good information on both sides would lead to good and lasting agreements. I was unconsciously practicing circular thinking long before I had a name for it. By the winter of 1988, I was reporting back to the First Nation on my findings.

To really understand what happened next, we have to know a bit about the early meetings between the British and Indigenous peoples in Canada.

In the late 1500s, the British landed on what they saw as *terra nullius*, now known as Canada, first as fishermen. Eventually they became excited about the colonizing potential. Indigenous people originally encountered the newcomers and welcomed them with an offer of friendship, in keeping with their more circular governance practices. Eventually, the shock of these two disparate mindsets led to conflict.

Fairly quickly, the harsh Canadian climate and the country's vastness, along with the fighting skills of the Indigenous peoples, convinced the British that accepting friendship was a good option. The British and Indigenous peoples of Eastern Canada entered into a unique style of agreement known as the Peace and Friendship Treaties. These treaties didn't record transactional land deals, as later treaties would. Instead, they affirmed the nature of the respectful relationship between the British and the Indigenous peoples. There was an underlying assumption that good relationships would lead to positive future outcomes, even though they had different understandings of what that would look like. It was a circular moment in Canadian history that some say extends its benefits into the present day.

Then a new problem of blurred lines around title presented itself to the British. The British definition of land ownership required "improvements". Indigenous peoples' lifestyle, which was in harmony with nature, didn't qualify. In addition, Indigenous peoples also welcomed trappers and traders. Sometimes these newcomers paid Indigenous people for plots of land to make homes for themselves. In the eyes of the British, these rogue "micro-colonies" were creating a huge land title issue.

Then someone had a brilliant idea. The Royal Proclamation (RP) of 1763 was being written to encourage early French settlers to stay in Canada under British rule. Why not include a few statements that recognized the Indigenous peoples of Canada as owners of their lands? This preserved their relationship under the Peace and Friendship Agreement. It also created the opportunity to make it illegal for Indigenous people to sell land to anyone but the Crown. Problem solved. The Crown had bought some time to complete treaty negotiations across Canada and assert sovereignty.

But treaty negotiations were an expensive and protracted business, even back then. By the 1880s, colonists had decided it would be way better if the Indigenous peoples just assimilated into the new Canadian culture.

The Crown offered a voluntary assimilation program. One Indigenous person in all of Canada signed up. Undaunted, the Crown used the *Indian Act* to try to regulate traditional activities such as potlatches and pow wows out of existence, cutting out the heart of Indigenous culture to support assimilation. The bug in the plan was that aboriginal rights and title are enshrined in the laws of Canada through the RP of 1763. Ever clever, in 1927 the Canadian government made it illegal for Indigenous people to hire a lawyer or for lawyers to advise on Indigenous rights without a licence from the superintendent general. Problem solved again, through the power of linear thinking.

That is, it was solved until 1951 when the tide of public sentiment shifted again. Nazi Germany's belief in a racial hierarchy had made Canadians more sensitive to human rights. Circular concepts like inclusion and diversity became popular, as they had been during the early peace and friendship days. The sections of the *Indian Act* blocking the assertion of aboriginal title and interests and the practice of traditional activities were repealed.

Fast-forward to 1988 and the Yukon comprehensive land claim and self-government negotiations. As mentioned earlier, these negotiations looked to the Harvard Negotiation Project and Roger Fisher and William L. Ury's book *Getting to Yes* (the same William Ury from the earlier example with Chechnya and Russia). The parties saw themselves as working together to solve the shared problems of treaty negotiations.

At the same time, Yukon First Nations were asked to draw

lines on a map that signified "mine" and "yours" within their traditional territories. This mismatch between circular and linear thinking created an invisible tension.

It was around this time that I stood in a community hall on the edge of a vast frozen lake, unfolding my geologic maps. I waited for people to brave the 40-below weather for our meeting, and in a few moments I would recommend zones of un-staked ground with theoretically elevated mineral potential. My lines on the map were based on interpretations of what the current science knew about the predictability of mineralization in their traditional territory. Presumably, this would inform my client's land selections. I was prepared to defend my recommendations in the face of tough questions.

Surprisingly, the Yukon First Nation participants first wanted to know about my family. Their comments on my work were appreciative, such as "Thank you for all the good work you have done for us," and "I really like your maps. Your colouring is excellent."

I particularly appreciated this last compliment. My massive hand-coloured compilation map was a work of art as well as science, but I hadn't expected anyone to notice. In this crowd, it was all about noticing. Not everyone may have understood the science. Many weren't even trying to understand the science because they cared about other values. They were determined that we have a connection on a human level.

I was experiencing the same Indigenous governance principles that settlers had encountered when they arrived and were welcomed. This drive to form a relationship was striking.

In the meetings I was used to participants attempted to poke holes in what I said, to objectively test the downside risks of my recommendations. This much different approach was generating benefits I had never imagined: I eventually felt so comfortable that I shared my sense of humour, and my clients laughed generously. They added their hunting stories and I ventured into analogies between hunting and prospecting. Gradually, we both understood inherent patterns and the possibility of any number of individual variations. Despite the barriers of geology terminology and cultural differences, we were having a rich conversation. Everyone in the room was engaged and sharing on unexpected levels. I began to think about exploration work and trapping practices more holistically – how they might support each other. The clients got a more relaxed version of me, and I was able to hear what they were showing me was of importance to them.

In this receptive room I was able to customize my presentation to their interests. In a linear environment, I would have intently focused on delivering and defending my findings (as I proved so expertly on that date that I didn't know I was on in Chapter 1).

When this introductory meeting concluded, nobody summarized future action items. I was shocked. The outcome of the meeting was that we had formed a respectful and sharing relationship.

The biggest impact of a circular meeting is what happens in the days and years that follow. The conditions were created for a long relationship of exchanged wisdoms and support. To this day I welcome seeing someone from that community who has found another interesting rock, wants to talk about prospecting experiences, or has a story to tell me, and I always learn something.

The First Nation used their land selections for several purposes: to protect and preserve culturally significant areas for future generations, to select lands that had some potential for their participation in economic benefits, and as an introduction to the nature of the mineral industry and how they would choose to form a relationship with it.

This experience has similarities with the lasting impacts the 16th- century Peace and Friendship Treaties had on Canada.

John Ralston Saul, co-chair of the Institute for Canadian Citizenship, wrote an opinion piece in *The Globe and Mail* with a headline that read: "A circle, edging ever outward: Canada's approach to immigration is the product of a long relationship with Indigenous peoples – and their concepts of inclusion, belonging, and balance." In this article, Saul suggests, "Canada at its best is very much the product of its long relationship with Indigenous peoples, their approaches and philosophies, which today we would call immigration and citizenship."

The circular practice of welcoming strangers, as seen when the Indigenous people of Canada initially welcomed the British, and when I was welcomed at that meeting by the frozen lake, has apparently found its way into Canadian policy today. There is a feeling in Canada that immigration and citizenship are inseparable steps. Immigrants are often encouraged to think of themselves as citizens upon arrival, receiving language lessons and ideally appreciation for the plurality, diversity, and interculturalism they bring. The image is of a fruitcake, not a melting pot. Other democratic countries often view immigrants as migrants, refugees, or guest workers who will someday return home.

Grand Chief John Kelly, in his testimony before the 1977 Royal Commission on the Northern Environment, said, "As the years go by, the circle of the Ojibway gets bigger and bigger. Canadians of all colours and religions are entering that circle. You might feel that you have roots somewhere else, but in reality, you are right here with us."

This kind of circular thinking is arguably one of the primary characteristics that makes Canada impressive today.

My experiences with this First Nation planted the seeds of my awareness of linear and circular thinking. As my curiosity grew, I turned to the latest scientific research. I was excited to discover that scientists were coming to very similar conclusions.

The Scientific Perspective

Antonio Damasio, a professor of neuroscience and neuro-biology at the University of Southern California, set out to understand how our minds make decisions. Damasio's research began with the historical lifetime medical records of a fellow named Phineas Gage. Gage's story is a cautionary tale of what happens when we fail to apply linear thinking when it is imperative. In 1848, he was a self-confident young railroad construction manager on a successful career track. He moved easily from technically demanding jobs to working well with people. We could say he had high linear and circular intelli-gence – until one day it all came to a screeching halt when he misjudged his optimal thinking mode.

Railroad bed blasting involved a strict sequence of events. A drilled hole was filled halfway with explosive powder and a fuse was inserted. The hole was then loaded with sand and a metal rod was used to tamp down the sand before the fuse was lit. This last step ensured the blast energy went into the rock and not out the hole. Gage was the one to take on the high-risk task of tamping down the sand.

While waiting for the sand to be loaded into one fateful blast hole, Gage turned for a moment to engage in a conversa-tion. Turning back to the job at hand, he placed the rod into the hole and tamped down on the explosive powder. The rod blasted out of the hole, through his cheek, out the top of his skull, and landed more than a hundred feet away. Gage had failed to notice the lack of sand. (This would never have hap-pened if he was firmly planted in linear thinking mode.)

Remarkably, Gage was still alive, and conscious. Quickly the crew helped him into a cart, and they careened towards town and the doctor's office.

When the doctor arrived, Gage was waiting on the front porch and is reported to have said, "Doctor, here is business enough for you." It must have seemed a bizarre use of comic understatement at the time. In fact, it was the first indication that Phineas Gage was locked in a rational state of mind, unable to access his social and relational powers.

Contrary to everyone's expectations, Gage recovered physically, as seen in this picture of him as a circus attraction, holding the thirteen-and-a-half-pound iron rod that had blasted through his brain. He was pronounced cured in two months, and in his physicality, he was healed, but his personality was never the same. His likes, dislikes, and aspirations were forever changed. Where once he was congenial, he was now fitful, used foul language, and lacked follow-through on plans. He was irreverent and indifferent to others. Over time, Gage was fired from his jobs, and all his relationships fell away.

Phyllis Gage Hartley,
Creative Commons

Two things have happened here. First, Gage is a cautionary tale for the perils of ignoring the principles of linear thinking when danger is afoot. Second, because of the specific way the rod blasted through his head, Gage had lost his emotional intelligence. This has become a seminal piece of information in neuroscience.

Damasio observed similar results in other patients who experienced varying degrees of damage to the same brain region. Their perception, memory, language, and intelligence remained intact but usually with one exception. These patients struggled with things like empathy, spotting potential for interpersonal conflict, responding to change, evaluating priorities, or avoiding bad options. Relationships and decision making became very difficult.

Expanding on this early insight, scientists have concluded that emotion plays a significant role in memory, perception, learning, reasoning, and navigating problems. It suggests our brains attach emotion to the information that impresses us. This information-emotion pairing supports what we remember.

This explains how we can stand on a busy street without being completely overwhelmed by the estimated eleven million pieces of information the brain can absorb each second. Neuroscientists suggest we selectively process about forty of these pieces of information for recall. Our emotional associations select what will be remembered by tagging some aspects with an emotion. These pieces of information are placed into our memory bank. The rest float by.

By this theory, emotional responses are filtering all the information we receive and determining what we will retain. Think about that for a moment. There is no such thing as an unemotional decision because all the information we have in our memory bank has an emotion attached to it. If information doesn't inspire an emotion, we don't remember it. And if we don't remember it, we don't use that information when we make a decision. Imagine seeing an early warning of a tsunami coming to our beach and watching it happen because we didn't attach an emotion to that bit of information.

It also means that if we experience an emotion there may be a belief attached, and we are being influenced by its limits or inspirations. Likewise, when a memory is recalled the associated feeling is activated. There is then the choice to get feelings under control or explore them for the sense of meaning and growth they can offer.

Damasio's research further determined that the emotions that get attached to selected information fall into two broad categories. Damasio referred to the two categories as feelings of pain and feelings of pleasure.

(This was exciting for me to read. There seemed to be a strong possibility that this was another way of describing linear and circular thinking.)

These categories, named pain and pleasure, were originally used by social scientist Jeremy Bentham (1748-1832). Bentham was a fascinating man who believed that the right thing to do was easily determined by asking yourself, "What will bring the most people happiness and the fewest people harm?"

This philosophy – known as utilitarianism – inspired Bentham to speak up for individual and economic freedom for men and women. He lobbied for the decriminalization of homosexuality, the right to divorce, the division of church and state, and freedom of expression all based on this principle. And he didn't stop there. He also spoke up for the abolition of slavery, the death penalty, and physical punishments for children. I'd say it proved to be an excellent guide for decision making.

Curiously, Bentham also wanted to be preserved as an auto-icon (a dead body preserved, dressed and displayed as if still living). This wish was granted. The first time I tried to visit him at University College London, his auto-icon was on tour to New York City. On my next visit, I was successful. He looks like a thoughtful and friendly guy.

Despite (or in addition to) this eccentricity, Bentham is broadly admired for his recognition that humans are driven by two broad categories of emotions that govern what we think, say, and do. In *The Principles of Morals and Legislation*, Bentham wrote, "Nature has placed mankind under the governance of two sovereign masters, pain and pleasure."

Damasio suggests that emotions of pain and pleasure create a kind of homeostasis for our thinking processes. Homeostasis is generally used to describe two opposite biological mechanisms that create a balanced internal state, despite external fluctuations. It is the reason we don't face problems like expanding like a puffer fish when we drink a glass of water and then looking like a dried prune an hour later.

We've long used this model for understanding biological functions, but it seems quite radical to apply it to our thoughts. Yet according to Damasio, sociocultural homeostasis has influenced our justice systems, economic and political organizations, the arts, medicine, and technology. From a bridge perspective, these are places where circular and linear thinking have found a balance point for current times.

Is it possible that emotions related to pain and pleasure are the complementary forces that create linear and circular thinking? Pleasure notices what is appealing and compels us to embrace it. Meanwhile, pain identifies what could be physically damaging to us and motivates us to push back against it. Between the two of them we can create well-being in the forms of comfort and safety (freedom from physical pain) and happiness (an internal experience of pleasure).

Several other scientists investigating how we think also propose two opposing mechanisms working to maintain optimal decision-making. Daniel Siegel, who has made a career of integrating brain science with psychology, describes two foundational mechanisms he calls survival and attachment modes. He says that the survival-focused brain is linear, literate, literal, and a list maker. It uses chains of logic, tends towards labelling things, and seeks cause/effect and if/then relationships. This survival drive has an on/off switch, which Siegel describes as an "or" point of view. Survival is a pain-avoidance mindset, which makes it compatible with Damasio and Bentham's pain category. It is also in strong alignment with my concept of linear thinking.

On the other hand, Siegel's attachment mode is described as a holistic mindset, and an image and metaphor-processing centre. It has an "and" point of view that comes from those brain functions that compel us to make connections. Attachment mode involves internal reflection, self-care, and soothing. It cares about meaning and relationships. It is not too much of a stretch to see attachment mode as related to pleasure, and circular thinking.

Scientific researchers are making a big point here. Several independent studies have recognized two distinct mindsets that team up to form our homeostatic thinking processes. Bentham and Damasio call them pleasure and pain drives, Siegel calls them attachment and survival mode, and Taylor calls them left and right brain thinking. The American cardiologists, Meyer Friedman and Ray H. Rosenman, who identified two personality types that related to the likelihood of getting heart disease, calls them Type A and Type B personalities.

I propose that the two drivers of human thought are best described as love-based and fear-based emotions. Here's why. Survival, pain, Type A, and left brain are all ways to describe the fear-based emotions related to linear thinking, while tactfully avoiding the association with emotion. However, the relationship to fear is a fundamental aspect that really helps us identify and use linear thinking. Not naming the emotion is a significant loss. Similarly, attachment, pleasure, Type B, and right brain are ways to describe the love-based emotions of circular thinking, while avoiding the use of the word "love."

What if recognizing the emotional roots of these two modes of thinking is the most important part of understanding them?

Emotional Intelligence Revisited

When I first read Daniel Goleman's book *Emotional Intelligence*, I found the stories intriguingly engaging. As time went by, though, I struggled to apply emotional intelligence in my own life. It seemed like the people in the book naturally knew what to do, and often, I could not translate that instinct to my situation. Once I saw that linear and circular thinking are rooted in fear-based and love-based emotions, it occurred to me that this is a framework for navigating situations using emotional intelligence. Each family of emotions (fear and love-based) activates a set of operating principles that are the keys to using emotional intelligence in a practical way. This suggests that when information is recalled, it arrives into one of two emotional worlds, each with its own unique operating principles.

Let's take a closer look at what I mean by fear-based and love-based emotions.

Fear-based Emotions

When a water pipe burst at my house, I felt anxious, and it didn't help when the insurance claims adjustor introduced himself as Allan Fear.

"Were you destined to this profession," I blurted, "or did your name push you into it?" (I'm a comedian when I'm stressed.)

He laughed and said, "I have a friend in the business named Frank Payne. We often joke about forming a company together."

There is no doubt that fear and pain go together. They are so closely linked that we often think of them as synonymous. But they are distinct.

This fascinates me.

Geneticist Paul Goldberg studies Congenital Indifference to Pain (CIP), a rare disorder in which individuals don't generate the emotion of fear in response to a sensation of pain. Edward H. Gibson was the first case of CIP ever recorded.

He worked in a circus in 1932, as The Human Pin Cushion. For his sideshow he was stuck with needles and showed no reaction. People with CIP describe how they can distinguish the difference between sharp and dull pain, or hot and cold sensations, but they are indifferent to them. They feel pain, but they don't respond with a fear-based emotion.

Children with CIP self-bite and burn themselves repeatedly because, without the fear typically associated with an experience of pain, they don't store fear-based memories. Consequently, they don't learn avoidance behaviours. As adults, they have multiple bone fractures that often heal badly because they lack the motivation that fear of a poor recovery gives us and sends us straight to the doctor for medical treatment. Tragically, when pain and fear are unlinked, much suffering and higher risk of mortality result.

Beyond first-hand experience of pain triggers, fear can be activated by visualizing a scenario like the pain of being in a car crash. This saves us from a lot of actual pain. The potential benefits of risk reduction motivate us to follow through with a safety plan. We don't have to experience a crash to realize it is a good idea to wear a seatbelt.

Furthermore, fear can be induced by others to motivate certain behaviours. Citizens not wanting to suffer negative consequences, like a ticket for not wearing a seatbelt, are also motivated to take preventative actions. Even without the physical sensation of pain, we can be motivated to take avoidance measures to prevent material losses such as a decline in social status or punitive financial costs. It is our fear-based emotions that are our ally in these situations of actual, virtual, and premeditated pain.

In this light, a few things become clear. Fear is not our enemy. Activating linear thinking through fear reduces the potential for pain and sometimes saves lives. When I first bought my house, I used my imagination and capacity to feel fear to recognize the potential for financial hardship if the house was damaged, so I bought insurance.

Interestingly, in linear thinking mode, our attention is focused on the source of our fear – something outside of us that we could take action against – rather than the feeling of fear itself. We experience the fear and immediately control our emotions while we take the information that has been highlighted and figure out an action plan that will reduce the possibility of pain. Fear drives us to work better, faster, smarter, or harder in order to win or survive.

If we were to slow the linear, fear-driven thinking process down to a snail's pace, the optimal broad pattern would look something like this: we keep our eyes up towards the horizon, scanning for an early warning of impending danger. Information portending an upcoming shortage of supplies, physical dangers ahead, an injustice that needs to be corrected, or a plot to do us harm is identified by a fear signal. Once our fear-activated emotions are triggered, linear thinking takes over to launch a countermove. If we are emotionally intelligent, we shut down our emotions, to avoid the pitfalls of over- or under-reacting. Then we gather all the relevant information, including a tally of available resources, apply logic, and devise an action plan. Bravery is not the absence of fear. It is the ability to control fear and take heroic actions.

Fear is activated in epic and mundane ways. Writing a daily to-do list is an action motivated by fear of losing focus or being unprepared. It greatly improves our chances of having a productive day. Project management breaks a big goal down into a series of manageable steps where the fear level can be controlled. Then we can focus on the work of ensuring each step is properly resourced and timed.

Budgets respond to the fear that resources will be squandered, and management software ensures no aspects of a project will be forgotten, as progress is tracked. The memory of a narrow escape due to a skill deficit motivates us to take more training. Risk assessments make a "go or no go" determination to ensure only projects with good odds of success are undertaken. In a war zone, fear sharpens our skills and accelerates our motivation. Fear can work for us in big and small ways. It starts by sending us into our linear thinking mode.

Although fear can be our ally, as described above, it can become a negative force if we fail to react appropriately.

What all these fear-activating situations have in common is that they alert us to a detrimental event coming from our external lives. This becomes important when we are trying to determine if our emotions are fear-based or love-based. Fear is activated by external motivations while love-based emotions respond to internal inspirations. This is the first important understanding for determining the appropriateness of linear or circular thinking mode.

Love-based Emotions

Love-based emotions are equal to fear in their ability to cause information to be remembered. Like fear-based emotions, they are collectively described in a few different ways. Bentham and Damasio called them "pleasure based." This sounds delightful but I wonder if it gives an overly euphoric impression of this range of emotions that also have a shadow side. Love-based emotions include feelings of longing, loneliness, despair, and low self-esteem. Seigel described this category of emotions as "attachment related," which feels more accurate, yet leans a bit too far towards mechanics rather than its psychological qualities for me. Love is what makes us distinctly human.

I prefer the term "love-based emotions" because we all

know love can bring joy and heartache. Also, fear and love are fine emotional counterpoints to each other.

Love-based emotions are the other half of what makes us whole. Imagine living in a world where you could only push back against what could cause pain. This second group of emotions are called upon by our internal impulse of feelings like joy, curiosity, engagement, and belonging. They compel us to pull in intriguing possibilities.

These two emotions speak differently. Fear grabs us when the external world signals danger, and shouts loudly for action. Love is a more subtle family of emotions. They have to be consciously received with a welcoming attitude. Only then can we awaken to the gifts that are presenting themselves. Curiosity, sorrow, delight, and discomfort draw us in and move us towards what might be possible. If we notice and trust them then novelty, insight, growth, and creativity become part of our lives. If we fail to respond to these feelings, ignore them, or allow fear to over-ride them, we are kicked into the linear world and our circular opportunities stagnate or fade away.

In the 1960s, researcher Louis Leakey wanted to radically change how research on primates was done. "Leakey was looking for a fresh pair of eyes and a fiery spirit – someone who could observe things that those in the existing scientific community were not able to do." He met Jane Goodall and was impressed with her open-mind, passion for knowledge, and a love of animals. She was also not scientifically trained. Goodall and her mother set up camp in the jungle, with the simple idea that they would live companionably beside the chimpanzees. Goodall wanted to experience chimpanzee society as a good neighbor. Her method was to observe, imitate, and take copious notes. She was severely criticized by scientists for giving chimpanzees names, and describing her perceptions of their feelings and personalities. Her intention was relational rather than being an objective observer of facts. Through her radical methods Goodall was able to make monumental discoveries that changed how humans understand themselves.

Whether it is wildlife, the environment, or another person, we make a connection through our emotions. This also guides the way life responds to us. Goodall chose a different emotional state, namely open-hearted curiosity instead of objectivity, and a radically different world was revealed to her. This circular approach could be a game changer.

Love-based feelings are authentically felt in the moment. We don't need to be told by experts, or have scientific proof when we know we like something. Our response is intuitive and body-felt, often benefiting from the full experience of smells, sounds, touches, tastes, and sights that inspire connections to our past, our imaginations, and our genuine nature. Love-based emotions provide us with a way of making meaning out of what has happened because they require moments of internal reflection.

Much to linear thinkers' chagrin, love-based emotions are dynamic. They are only required to be authentic in the moment. We don't know where our feelings will lead us, only that they are to be reflected on and trusted.

Love-based emotions hold energy. The natural ebb and flow of that energy informs us. When something we were engaged with no longer holds energy for us, we honour that by going back to the last connection-infused moment and looking around for the direction that re-energizes us. It is a courageous step into the unknown, nurtured by a sense of growing self-connection and trust. This is how cracks form in the predictable and the way we live our lives and structure our organizations is transformed. Love-based emotions support dynamic, resilient, and abundant environments in this way.

People often say that they can't think of an example of a love-based emotion that they would willingly bring into a governance or business conversation. But words like inclusion, resilience, empowerment, creativity, engagement, cross-cultural awareness, purpose, and vulnerability (thank you, Brené Brown) are becoming important organizational considerations. They all relate to emotional states of connection. Disconnection-related emotions such as exclusion, toxic culture, stagnation, boredom, and shame are also rooted in love-based emotions, on the shadow side (which we will explore in Chapter 4).

Here is a sampling of fear and love-based emotions as seen through the bridge framework. Each word can be prefaced with the phrase "I feel", Notice how fear-based emotions are triggered by external information and love-based are related to subjective ways of being:

FEAR-BASED EMOTIONS		LOVE-BASED EMOTIONS	
brave	cowardly	resilient	reckless
capable	controlled	curious	numb
efficient	distracted	engaged	lonely
ambitious	lazy	inspired	despondent
confident	afraid	playful	unwelcome
competitive	unmotivated	passionate	depressed
justified	misjudged	authentic	ashamed
loyal	disappointing	loved	jealous
righteous	wronged	empathetic	unforgiving
serious	guilty	grateful	envious
organized	irresponsible	happy	sad

Awkward Discoveries

Love Can Hurt

There is a pretty good chance that you are feeling some discomfort with the term "love-based emotions." I once tried to refer casually to love-based emotions at a geology meeting, and I blushed. In the Western world, the word "love" is strongly associated with romantic love. But the Greeks recognized six kinds of love: *philia*, the love for a brother, friend, or family; *ludus*, for playful love; *philautia*, to describe love of self; *eros*, after the god of sexual desire; *pragma*, the realistic long-term form of love, and *agape*, the love of our community and our planet.

As we face issues such as climate change, severe social problems, and pandemics, we need words that call up these broader understandings of love. When New Zealand's prime minister Jacinda Ardern famously responded to the massacre of Muslims by a white supremacist with the inspiring words, "Be kind, be strong," she chose a word that evokes *agape*, love that expands beyond self to encompass the entire country as a place of belonging. The issues of today often benefit from leadership that is not resistant to calling upon this love-based perspective.

Circular leadership aims to humanize processes, welcoming genuine and often awkward conversations. We don't know what will come from this process or where we will take it once an insight arrives. We enter into this conversation with respectful and open hearts, trusting that the result is often the discovery of something meaningful.

At Yukon First Nation general assemblies I have attended, the opening, closing, and event part of the middle of meetings are spent activating love-based emotions. At first, when I was only familiar with linear processes, I recall my levels of discomfort rising as the hours ticked by and the agenda remained untouched by noon on the first day. As the meetings unfolded, I learned that time spent noticing the beauty of the surroundings, catching up on what is happening in each other's communities, and enjoying dancing, singing, and playing games together inspired feelings of connection among the participants. Some may be remembering how they love to dance, or feeling the contagious happiness of another person, or having a sorrowful memory of a lost relative who danced beautifully. This ability to be connected while experiencing a range of feelings reminds people that they can have different feelings while facing the same situation. This is as true for joyful times as it is for difficult issues.

In the 1990s, Council of Yukon First Nations Grand Chief Harry Allen always started a general assembly by talking about how much love he felt for everyone there. He asked participants to approach their jobs with love and to listen to each other with open hearts. Towards the end, I saw how these statements set a powerful tone that reverberated in the background for the three-day meetings. People seemed predisposed to listen receptively and reach towards each other to find inclusive resolutions. Allen had removed any awkwardness about talking from the heart by modelling it in the opening moments of the gathering.

If saying "love-based" leaves you feeling ironically disconnected from the people in the room, try "connection-based emotions." Love is all about the ways we experience connection, including disconnection and reconnection.

Masculine-Feminine Dilemma

As I was developing this theory of linear and circular thinking, I noticed another pattern of word choice that is somewhat socially awkward to talk about. Many have suggested to me that there is a masculine and feminine parallel to linear and circular thinking. Let me first say that masculine is not the same as male, and feminine is not exclusively female. In this theory we all have a masculine and feminine side, whether we identify as male, female, non-binary, or LBGTQ, for example.

The NPR podcast *Invisibilia* had an interesting episode called "The New Norm" that told the story of Shell building the Ursa deepwater drilling project. In 1997, Shell set out to build a $1.5 billion oil rig the size of two football fields. It was their most ambitious deepwater drilling project to date. It required a huge shift in the oil industry's ways of operating. They had to learn to go from a routine operation run by 20 people on land to a 400-person site, atop 4,000 feet of open sea, using new technology. So many moving parts, so many things that could explode, so far from land.

Rick Fox was put in charge of the project. He began his career as a self-described country boy working as a rough-neck on little drilling platforms and he rose all the way to upper management. He was in a culture that knew fear, and enforced the unwritten macho rules of the industry such as these:

– never question authority;
– if you make a mistake, hide it;
– if you don't know how to do something, fake it;
– never appear weak; and above all,
– swallow your emotions.

These rules were somewhat effective in the stable, known conditions of land-based rigs. On the dynamic ocean with new large-scale technology, these rules were a recipe for disaster. Shell knew they had to do something different to be better prepared for what they were facing, but they were surprised to learn that it meant training men to be so comfortable with each other that they could cry.

It all started one day while Fox was contemplating drill schedules, production calendars, and hardware. He received a cold-call from Claire Nuer, the founder of a leadership coaching company called Learning as Leadership (LAL). Nuer wanted to offer Shell her leadership coaching services in preparation for this exceptional project. Fox accepted an exploratory meeting. As Fox describes the meeting, they met and he set out to explain the physical aspects of the project. Claire – a tiny, 64 years old, bejewelled-eyeglass-wearing Parisian, as well as a Holocaust and cancer survivor, interrupted him to say, "You are not talking real. And that's what you need... (What is it) that you are not allowing yourself to be open with? Can we just cut the B.S.? Because it is scary what you are doing... If you don't tell people you are scared, you are not going to be able to create safety together."

Fox hired LAL, and for the one and a half years of project construction, the people leading and managing Ursa underwent a series of workshops. These hyper-masculine oilmen thought the workshops were "silly" but they showed up as instructed. As they progressed, they felt vulnerable (not in a welcome way), and even hostile. Comments like, "Why would I share my personal feelings with people I barely know?" and "What has this got to do with oil?" were put forward as blocks. Still, little by little, the men kept doing the exercises. One day the exercise was to draw a timeline of their life and take turns standing up to talk about it. At first, men were focused on how to say the bare minimum. Then someone shared something real, and the whole dynamic shifted. The next man shared that his son was dying. He began to cry. That man fully expected to be teased as a crybaby but that never happened. This stuck with him. An emotional structure was developing where it was okay to have and share feelings.

Robin Ely of Harvard Business School heard of the LAL work with Shell and decided to study the impacts. She found there was an 84% decline in the company's accident rate after this learning culture was established. Productivity (number of barrels, and measures of efficiency and reliability) exceeded the previous industry benchmark.

It turns out that when workers are more open with each other emotionally, information flows in new ways. Technical information naturally finds places to be useful as people seek to make connections. They know when others are looking for support and want to offer it where they can. People readily admit mistakes, which provides an opportunity for everyone to learn. They reach out when they need help lifting something and ask when they don't know how to do something. Leadership shares the issues that they are struggling with and receives good information. They share thoughts with others who have grappled with similar issues. Workplace cultural norms are developed that make people comfortable with emotions. This learning culture smooths out operations and increases safety.

In linear thinking mode, emotions are controlled and logic takes over. People instinctively work to preserve and protect the status quo. Contrastingly, in circular thinking mode, feelings are welcomed and explored as people face the unknown. Gut instinct is trusted, along with group wisdom without logic or research to back it up. New actions are given a try.

When projects are complex, with lots of unpredictable interactions, these circular qualities are high functioning. Rather than preserving the image of being all-knowing, technically infallible, emotionally detached, physically tough guys, workers need to eagerly admit mistakes, ask questions, listen to the answers, and talk about their feelings.

The NPR host Hanna Rosen asked, "Is the moral of the story that, in order to succeed in the 21st century, it is better to choose an emotional structure that's girlie?" Talking about feelings, crying at work, willingness to admit mistakes: these are behaviours generally associated with women, are they not?

When the drilling executives were asked, "Were you teaching more female norms of interacting with each other?' they were shocked by the idea. They thought of it as opening up and becoming more themselves.

This is a description of the power of circular thinking; know yourself and be yourself. Perhaps it would be more useful to call the shift in behaviour of these oil men as a move from linear to circular thinking. These men have walked the distance from self-admitted hyper-masculinity to being so connected to their circular mode they can express a full range of emotion at work. However, asking them to call it a feminine transformation was pushing them too far.

Perhaps the point is that the oil men didn't need to categorize what they experienced in masculine/feminine terms to know they preferred this new way of being. Doing so actually creates a barrier for men to practice circular thinking. The men simply said it was much more fun. And the improved safety was impressive.

We could say that emotional self-awareness, and feminine ways of being are both subcategories of circular thinking. Furthermore, it could be said that circular thinking is the opposite of hyper-masculinity that is an extreme version of linear thinking.

At the same time, it was a woman who led the Shell executives to know how to be this way in the world. Nuer had learned to trust her felt experience through her journey with cancer. She used this insight to develop her unique approach for the Shell executives' workshops. It may be fair to say that women find it easier (be it rooted in biology or culture) to access circular thinking and trust emotions, be vulnerable, and depend on relationships. It may be more natural to them, but everyone is capable of both circular and linear thinking.

During WWII a special unit, the centre of code breaking operations, was headed by Dillwyn "Dilly" Knox and operated out of Bletchley Park. Knox had been an expert in literary papyri (Egyptian, Greek, Roman text written on papyrus). This fostered his talent for recognizing metric and rhythmic patterns.

One of this unit's tasks was to crack the code of a machine called Enigma. The machine had four windows with a wheel of letters under each one. The operator was to set each wheel with a randomly chosen letter, creating many millions of possible coded variations for the message to be sent. The allies code-breaking unit had teams of men largely considering the mathematical probabilities, and women who had a variety of skills including a deep knowledge of German poetry.

The women worked by strokes of imagination and intuition, and most importantly psychology. As described in Virginia Nicholson's book *Millions Like Us*, 21-year-old Mavis Batey recalled how one of them dreamt the combination and she was right! Batey further recounts that one of their team's successful techniques was to get to know the German operators of the Enigma machines because, despite German instructions to choose random letters, human nature meant the operators often chose four letter combinations like swear words or their girlfriends' names.

Batey's husband was a decoder in the men's team and she tells this story of the difference between the units:

Keith Batey, my husband, had trained to be a mathematician: we met at Bletchley. And I remember one occasion when I was tackling something. Keith looked over my shoulder and said, "The chance of you getting that out are four million to one against you." Well at coffee time I walked over to him, and with the greatest of pleasure I told him: "That came out in five minutes."

What if honed intuition, trust in our dreams, and following gut instinct is a valuable part of our decision-making powers? I wondered if there is a resistance to admitting that a circular approach, especially when seen as feminine, could be value-added to an operating system because it is the antithesis of linear thinking.

I vividly recall seeing an episode of *Star Trek* when I was about nine years old. Spock, Captain Kirk, Bones, and a woman were in a circle, strategizing their best move for tackling yet another interplanetary conflict. The guys were intently listening to the woman. This intrigued me, but I was gobsmacked when it became evident that the woman's contribution to the discussion was her feminine intuition. Not only did the team respect her insight, but they then proceeded to make a plan that included her perspective. I remember thinking that this is what the future would look like: two different ways of interpreting the world, working together.

In the mining industry, the heroic impulse often compels men to launch linear protections that ensure safe participation of women in male-dominant environments. In the effort to be more inclusive of women, the focus is on prevention of women's victimization, as they operate in male-dominated linear systems. This is important.

It is also important to recognize the value added by incorporating the circular perspective that many women operate from into the workplace – namely the ability to ask questions, share emotions, work holistically, follow intuition, and admit mistakes to gain learning opportunities.

People who are comfortable with their circular side often find themselves living in an environment where all things linear are exalted. By default, their instinct to use emotions as a resource is viewed as a flaw.

There are many women who master linear processes in the workplace by accessing skills typically associated with masculinity. I hope I proved to have a measure of these in my field geology career as I used a chain saw, observed helicopter safety protocols, and built outhouses. At the same time, I kept my circular perspective secret in order to fit in. If a group doesn't have language for the methods and benefits of diverse thinking modes, some group members remain invisible or are disparaged for being different from the dominant perspective.

In a business setting, Dai Lu's boss, Kent, included her in a session with their clients. After the meeting, he asked for her thoughts. "I noticed there is tension between Sam and Sharon," Dai Lu offered. "They seem very guarded with each other. Also, Sharon usually has a lot to say, but Sam dominated the conversation. Sharon seemed subdued."

Kent couldn't understand what Dai Lu was talking about. It sounded like she was making a seating plan for a social event.

"You need to focus on the things that matter to your job. Please limit your comments to project-related aspects in the future," he instructed, hoping to improve her future contributions. Dai Lu felt rebuffed and learned to keep her relational observations to herself. Meanwhile, within a month, Sharon left her position, taking her expertise with her, and the project stalled. Dai Lu stayed with Kent's company, but the company never benefitted from her talent for relational insights. Daiu Lu shaped her behaviour to match Kent's worldview and improve her opportunities for promotion.

Circular leadership is needed to create practices that support the flourishing of circular thought within a dominantly linear environment. Otherwise, introduction of circular methods will consistently be dismissed as inappropriate. Partially formed circular ideas will be seen as the opposite of a good idea before they have a chance to evolve.

Logic is Not a Panacea

Rational thought, logic, and reason are essential to linear thinking, which has fear-based emotions at its foundation. (It often surprises people that logic is fear-based. In Chapter 5 we will notice how logic is used to push back against unwanted behaviours, and is rooted in either/or decisions which are hallmarks of activation of the family of fear-based emotions and linear thinking.) Therefore, rational thought must be suspended to access circular thinking. Many people find this shocking at first. However, to switch from linear to circular thinking we have to put our linear operating systems on pause long enough to make room for love-based emotions and the associated circular thinking practices. This is not always easy to do. Having the concept of the bridge between two thinking styles provides the neutral between space.

Except in the case of violent interactions, fear and the associated linear thinking are not the optimal mindset for inter-personal conflict resolution. This means concepts like logic, rational thought, and reason need to be set aside in times of relationship breakdown because of their requirement to get control over our emotions. This becomes a really important point when we recognize that choosing fear-based words sends us into the entire set of linear operating principles including push back and be objective. In no time, relationship trust becomes collateral damage.

Abraham Heschel, a leading twentieth-century Jewish theologian and philosopher, captured the situation by saying, "The search for reason ends at the shore of the known: on the immense expanse beyond it, only the sense of the ineffable can glide... Citizens of two realms, we all must sustain a dual allegiance." As soon as we are in unpredictable and unprecedented situations, we must be aware that circular thinking just became our best option.

A lawyer named Sarah flew into a village in the high Arctic

to meet with her Indigenous clients. She was met by her guides and outfitted in sealskin clothing for the continued journey to her meeting place by dog-team.

"You may rest now, and we will leave after sunset," the guide said.

"Why not travel now?" Sarah queried, logically questioning why they would waste time.

The guide paused, and then nodded. They were on the trail just after noon. Every step was arduous as the man-and-dog teams broke through the surface crust into thigh-deep snow. It was like perpetual stair-climbing, with the addition of a blinding glare coming off the snow.

The hours crawled by until mercifully the sun sank below the horizon. The temperature dropped, the surface crust hardened, and the dog-teams sped across the snow and towards the village where Sarah's meeting would occur.

Sarah was shocked that the guides had not simply told her it was better to travel at night. In trying to make sense of it, she wondered if, because she was white, or because she was a lawyer, they had deferred to her opinion as the top of a perceived hierarchy (a fear-based structure).

Perhaps, but another possible interpretation is that in circular thinking mode the meaning behind our actions is highly significant. Finding this meaning requires experience and a period of reflection before that "aha" moment sinks in. By offering a logical option based on time efficiency Sarah was inadvertently disrespecting the wisdom of locals. Maybe the guide decided the answer would be most meaningful if it came through experience. Rather than explaining the physical properties of snow, which logically would have made their trip a lot easier for them all, the guide was showing Sarah that if she arrived in the Arctic willing to listen and learn from local wisdom, she'd have an easier ride. This was a gift that would keep giving throughout her work with her Indigenous clients if she was able to read the message. If this was his message, I am sure it was delivered with the intention of helping her to grow into all that she is capable of being.

In circular mode, it is important to listen and receive, so we can experience what other people have to offer. This means giving up the linear quest for alignment with logic and progress, and instead assuming a 360° perspective to take in all the possible directions the other person may be offering.

When we have a one-world view, we always default to our most comfortable thinking mode, and often that is linear. If we pause to question this, we might find another way forward.

Can relational conflict be resolved through linear measures like contracts, payment, wars, or new laws? Is the answer to climate change to push back against the symptom of danger (by legislating against a rise in temperature) or the call for a global psychological revolution where we envision ourselves as living in harmony with the cycles of nature? It will feel awkward to set logic aside for a period of time and reach towards people's hearts and imaginations but the potential gains are worth the trouble.

Chapter 4
Power

What is power?

It is an important question to have a ready answer for, because every decision we make is rooted in our concept of power.

Prior to this project, I didn't give it much thought, mostly because everything I read and heard seemed to align with a single concept of power. Essentially it is synonymous with control.

With the development of the bridge, I started to wonder. If there are two ways of knowing, and they are radically different from each other, wouldn't that also mean there are two concepts of power?

Imagine that – double the power.

Linear Power

From Oxford to Merriam-Webster, the definitions of power are versions of achieving control over variables to shape a preferred outcome. I like the clarity put forward at the turn of the nineteenth century by German philosopher, sociologist, and political economist, Max Weber. He defined power as essentially:

To realize one's own will, even against resistance.

According to Weber, this linear power comes in two forms.

One version of linear power is authoritative. In this version of power, people agree to submit to the laws and requirements of governments, employers, or other institutions in exchange for services or benefits. In the movie *The Perfect Storm*, for example, the family clinging to their sailboat during the mother of all horrific storms was glad that they had agreed to submit to the authoritative power of the US government in exchange for the excellent services of the air-sea rescue team. For their part, the government brought excellence to their services in order to secure the compliance of their citizens.

These same opportunities to gain authoritative linear power exist in a well-executed engineering project. This realm is about building predictability into systems through regulation, lines of authority, and proven practices.

The other form of linear power is coercive, and anyone who has seen an action movie knows this variation of power. For example, when Luke Skywalker and his allies are pushing back against evil to save the Empire in *Star Wars*, that's coercive power. We're rooting for Luke to assert his will, despite Darth Vader's evil resistance. Simultaneously, Vader is using his linear power to crush Luke and his allies. What we have here is a pushing match. The team with the greatest pushing power, cleverest strategy, and strength of will wins.

The difference between being a winner or a loser in this competition of wills is a heads-up attitude, scanning the horizon for early signs of incoming danger and obstacles; a network of strong allies; efficient use of resources; and the strength of a top-notch skilled team, all pulling in the same direction with determination.

Linear power can be awe inspiring, like in the depiction of the operating systems of an air-sea rescue team in *The Perfect*

Storm. It was a magnificent moment when the rescue helicopter blade sliced through the raging rain and wind to reach the capsized sailboat. As two rescue workers stepped out of the helicopter into the perilously icy waters like it was just another day at the office I gasped. Instantly their jumpsuits became flotation devices and the reassuring voice of their pilot came through their helmets. This wasn't their first rodeo. Countless procedural and technical equipment development hours went into giving these men a fighting chance against formidable dangers. As a result, they successfully asserted their will to bring that family home, with distinction. That's linear power at its best – through research, product development, planning, and adherence to accepted emergency service protocols, the rescuers were able to overcome dangers and rescue citizens.

We call on linear power in big and small ways every day. I recently traveled to Europe for a meeting. Upon my arrival in the airport, I scanned for information that would get me to my hotel and on to my meeting in a timely fashion.

A sign read, "Welcome to Bonn." Panic flashed through me – my meeting was in Cologne.

"Bring it under control," I told myself. "Assess the situation, gather more intel."

Within 15 minutes I'd learned that Cologne and Bonn share an airport, and that Cologne is also spelled Koln. The next sign didn't scare me at all. Each step of the way, I became more skilled in this foreign land and more capable of asserting my will to get to my meeting on time.

The Goldilocks Test

It's not too hard to see how asserting your will, even against resistance, could lead to antisocial behaviour or excessive collateral damage. At the other extreme, not enough effort results in being bested by the person who brought their

A-game. To avoid these shadow sides of linear power, we need this Goldilocks Test to find the optimal zone:

Not too much, not too little, just right.

In essence, the middle zone is good and the extremes in either direction are bad. This often results in a bell-curve of behaviour.

Linear leaders know the motivational power of conveying the consequences of failure to their teams. It adds urgency and intention to the task at hand. However, it's essential to find that middle zone. Too little pressure is weak leadership, too much results in tyranny.

That "just right" zone assessment depends on knowing the real-world consequences of not meeting deadlines and reaching milestones. With this information, team members can prioritize conflicting goals and put in the hours needed to complete tasks. However, if there is a constant stream of urgent projects it becomes overwhelming, and the result is burnout. Also, excessive fear may cause people to practice avoidance, denial, or blame tactics. Another consequence of excessive use of fear motivators is teams that become overly competitive, to the degree of hiding information, using excessive force, or undermining other's efforts. Over-estimation of the required actions can also produce the unintended consequence of a highly motivated competitor fuelled by righteous indignation.

Most organizations have mechanisms like policies, rules, budgets, engineering standards, and professional codes that define the boundaries of "too much" or "too little." Governments use laws, and regulations to perform this function.

There are optimal times for linear power. For example, when an external force is intent on doing us harm in order to achieve its goal, a wilful drive to block it is required. As Churchill said, "An appeaser is one who feeds a crocodile hoping it will eat him last." We cannot ignore the fact that the crocodile is firmly in a predatorial mode and will always see us as food. We need to take preventative action rather than work with the crocodile.

Garry Kasparov, the world chess champion who challenged Vladimir Putin for Russian leadership, explores the risks of not taking up linear power when it is needed in his book, *Winter is Coming*. Kasparov describes the decision-making of modern world powers in this way:

> Instead of standing on principles of good and evil, of right and wrong, and the universal values of human rights and human life, we have engagement, resets, and moral equivalence...[We] must fight with the vast resources of the free world, beginning with moral values, and economic incentives, and with military action only as a last resort.

Kasparov recognizes that dangerous intent exists in the world and needs to be combatted with appropriate amounts of linear power. The big question is: How do we find that "just right" zone?

In the sports arena, players compete to realize their will

against the resistance of the other team, within the rules of the game. It's that last part that I find most interesting. Working within the rules of the game is where integrity, self-discipline, skill, and discernment are on display. In other words, the Goldilocks Test is being played out to find that "just right" zone as teams push to the edge of their ability. It's awe-inspiring to see the players use their skills to score goals while simultaneously adhering to the rules of authoritative power and self-monitor their use of coercive power.

When authoritative power fails to adequately define "too much," it is entirely up to the players to have a super-human ability to control their level of coercive actions.

In a hockey game between the Vancouver Canucks and the Colorado Avalanche in February 2004, rookie centre Steve Moore delivered a blow to the head of Vancouver captain and league top scorer Markus Näslund. Näslund suffered a minor concussion and a bone chip in his elbow. Delivering pain like this is intended to throw off a superstar's game with the hope the heightened fear of pain might instinctively cause a player to shy away from becoming a target again. In a press conference, seasoned players demanded justice – Moore had broken the unofficial player code against targeting a skilled player with a vicious body check or "cheap shot." (I was surprised by this deference to a hierarchy based on skill level.)

The existing authoritative power, in the forms of the referee and the National Hockey League, responded by deeming Moore's hit legal. A big zone opened up for the use of linear power on the ice.

The Canucks were incensed and players indicated there would definitely be a price on Moore's head, signaling that they were prepared to deliver retribution as a deterrent.

A few weeks later, the Canucks and Avalanche faced each other on the ice again. Canucks' defenseman Todd Bertuzzi set out to provoke Moore into a fight.

Emotions were running high throughout the arena, heightened by the score being eight to two for the Avalanche. When Moore wasn't provoked to fight, Bertuzzi grabbed Moore's jersey from behind, punched him in the head and landed on him. The other Canucks players dogpiled on top as the crowd cheered enthusiastically.

As the pile disassembled, Moore lay unconscious on the ice, his face lacerated from the unprotected fall and his neck damaged in two places, possibly from the dogpile.

The crowd went silent. The big screen showed Bertuzzi's shocked expression when he saw that Moore was not getting up.

How much is too much effort to create a deterrent? The league, Bertuzzi, and his team failed to find the optimal zone, and it cost Bertuzzi and Moore. Bertuzzi was criminally and civilly charged, and suspended for seventeen months. While on the road after his return, he was constantly heckled and booed by fans.

In 2010, a new rule was introduced by the NHL, stating that any form of "lateral or blindside hit to an opponent, where the player's head is targeted and/or the principal point of contact (known as an illegal check to the head) is prohibited." This rule is specific, measurable, applicable to all players, and gives clear advance direction. These are the hallmarks of strong authoritative direction for finding the acceptable zone for the use of linear power.

With or without the authoritative rules, the players also had the responsibility to apply the Goldilocks Test when they used their coercive power. It requires enormous discipline in the heat of the moment.

This quest for that "just right" zone often benefits from authoritative power taking a long-term view. During times of calm, the bigger goals of safety, morality, and success can be strategized. In moments of high stress, rigid adherence to the plan increases the potential to achieve those longer-term goals.

The Goldilocks Test applies equally to business when fear is the driving emotion: fear of missing a deadline, losing a competition with another business, losing the support of allies, or going over budget. The Goldilocks Test helps us find the right amount of effort for applying coercive and authoritative linear power.

It is also important to note that linear power is appropriate when the assumption of predictability is correct, and in response to an external danger. Otherwise, we need to look for another form of power.

Circular Power

The use of linear power is so prevalent that I found myself wondering if power is strictly a linear concept.

The title of Adam Kahane's 2010 book *Power and Love: A Theory and Practice of Social Change* (which I loved) suggests that love is something other than a source of power. Then a song on the radio caught my attention. It was Huey Lewis and the News singing "The Power of Love." Now, Mr. Lewis was definitely not celebrating his ability to assert his will over the lucky recipient of his affection. He was singing of the energizing feelings of passion, purpose, and empowerment that accompany love – that drive to do something for the pure joy of connection to self and to another. Listening to the song reminds us that love has a unique power of its own.

I became obsessed with finding a description for this form of power that was all about connections. Otherwise, every time power was summoned, only linear power would step forward.

Finally, I found an understanding of power, once prevalent among ancient cultures, that is becoming increasingly relevant again today. It is seen in the inscription "Know Thyself" carved, in Greek, of course, in the forecourt of the Temple of the Oracle of Delphi in Greece. It is also found in the words of Socrates, supposedly delivered during his trial for impiety and corrupting youth, when he said, "An unexamined life is not worth living." (As the story goes, Socrates' connection to his words was so strong that he preferred death over denying their truth. He was subsequently executed.)

These statements evoke the essence of this second kind of power. I found that, as it was applied by the Greek philosophers and throughout history, all the way up to today's social media influencers, circular power can be accessed through the phrase:

> Know yourself, be yourself,
> and support others in doing the same.

This is a radically different concept of power. It is rooted in an internal gaze where we find self-awareness and become conscious of our power over the way we respond to our feelings and the evolution of our beliefs. It is in this thinking mode that we find sources of meaning, our self-esteem, happiness, and a connection to our innate talents and interests. It leads to governments intent on empowering citizens, and to purpose-driven businesses. With this power, people learn to be in the world with ever-greater authenticity and follow a quest to bring their best selves to life.

Know Yourself

Sophie Flather, a young Vuntut Gwitchin woman, lives in the remote Yukon community of Old Crow. Her village of about 300 people, located above the Arctic Circle, is reached by plane or a multi-day paddle or ski-doo down the Eagle and Porcupine Rivers. The long, sharply cold winters mean people spend a considerable amount of time inside, literally and figuratively, including time with their own thoughts.

Flather summarized her role in the community by saying, "Everything starts with yourself. To be part of a healthy community you have to be healthy in yourself. I try to be responsible for myself."

It is a powerful leadership choice to take the time to know ourselves and to model bringing that self-knowledge into the gatherings we attend by communicating with appropriate authenticity.

In the 2021 online series *Reconciling Ways of Knowing*, Session 8, Leah George-Wilson explains why she introduces herself by saying, and then translating from her language, the following:

> Greetings to honoured guests and Dear Ones. I have good feelings in my heart to see all of you today. In our language, hən̓q̓əmin̓əm̓, I told you my name, who my parents are, and who my grandparents are because in our way, that information is important for you to know, so that you know that I know exactly who I am. In our world these things are important.

George-Wilson is showing that she is a person who is capable of generating the circular power of knowing herself, being herself, and supporting others in doing the same.

By their example, circular leaders encourage others to take the time to know themselves. This process supports the letting go of inherited triggers that are no longer useful. Emotional room is created to reconnect to what we would genuinely like to offer to our work and life. Self-doubt is gradually replaced with a healthy sense of entitlement to take up space and participate in life. In this inclusive environment, each person's interests, talents, and authentic views become worthy of attention. People can accept their whole selves and choose what they will share with others.

Since beginning this book I have given more value to knowing what is meaningful and joyful to me. I have learned that I experience happiness when sharing all aspects of sauna culture with family and friends. A warm beverage on a cold morning grounds me, and strong mental health for myself and others is a value worth aspiring to. These are some of my places of connection to self. No matter how difficult my day, I can change my mood by engaging in these activities actually or through my imagination, or remembering past events.

Linear thinking is about doing, while in the circular world we care about our way of being in the world. Here we awaken to our emotions, beliefs, and imaginations. With curiosity we own all aspects of ourselves, and take responsibility for what we bring to all our relationships, including to our self-talk.

Be Yourself

Circular thinking pays attention to the art of being in relationship with others and our environment. It graciously accepts where we are now, and seeks insight into what parts of ourselves we want to express in the world. Finding the courage to be ourselves, with all its vulnerability, is a step towards generating the circular power of becoming our best version of ourselves.

Lana Eagle, a consultant to the mineral exploration and mining industry, told a story at a gathering on social licence to operate that I attended. Eagle recalled a workshop where an elder visited from person to person, taking a moment to talk with each one. She noticed that she was feeling nervous as her turn approached. Raised outside of her culture, Eagle worried she might be seen as being out of place.

When the elder reached her, he simply asked her how she was doing.

"I'm a bit nervous," she said honestly.

The elder laughed and said, "All you have to do is start where you are, and we'll see how far we can go."

Eagle felt herself relax. The elder's advice contains a profound message that each of us is already all we need to be in this moment. Our effort will be enough, and we know enough to make a valuable contribution.

The phrase, "start where you are, and see how far you can go," transports us to circular thinking mode – a place free of fear of group expectations or the quest for comparative excellence. When I feel overwhelmed, I often tell myself to simply start where I am. I find it remarkable how this reminder grounds me and encourages me to share what I am experiencing.

In a workshop I led for a government department on how to participate in a circular meeting, we arranged the tables in a round formation. I invited everyone to make themself comfortable during the day and said, "To start we are going to go around the circle and give each person a moment to reflect and share some thoughts on how they are feeling and what makes a good work culture. If it comes to your turn and you feel you are not ready to share, I hope you will feel comfortable enough to honor that." I took in a slow breath, and said, "My first thought is how nice it is to be here with all of you this morning. And to have the cinnamon buns! Thank you to the people who brought those in. So good. This might be the largest circular meeting I have led. I'm curious to see how it goes, and mostly excited to hear people's thoughts on their work culture." I paused here. "That's mostly what's going on for me right now." Then I turned to my left for the next person to do the same kind of reflection.

In this way, each person had a moment to share their thoughts. Around the table, seasoned workers, new managers, and students in their first month on the job took their turn and shared their impressions of their job. When we reached a shy young woman who had joined the department only a month ago, we paused while she looked conflicted. I had to hold myself back from rescuing her by repeating that she could pass. Then she said something like, "As my turn was getting closer, I was experiencing some dread. But now that it is my turn to talk, there is actually a calmness in being here. It's nice not to have to worry about being cut off or contradicted. Instead of worrying that what I say won't be smart enough, I can share what I'm wondering or noticing. I'm surprised, but I actually like this." After a pause, she had questions from her beginner's mind. Subsequent speakers started talking about the unspoken guidelines that make it possible to do their work and the conversation suddenly became very interesting.

These were really intriguing points. How many ideas are suppressed because the speaker does not thrive in a competitive environment? It is actually common for fledgling ideas to need an atmosphere of acceptance, with an eye towards possibilities rather than a spotlight on flaws. A circular meeting creates this environment. We also saw the gain that comes from admissions of confusion. Circular leadership encourages these kinds of insights.

Support Others in Knowing and Being Themselves

Beyond knowing ourselves and being ourselves, circular power is generated by the desire to support others in their quest for growth, for the simple joy of seeing someone else find fulfillment. As a happy consequence of our circular efforts, unexpected spin-off benefits often occur such as happiness, meaningful work, an expansive sense of community, and communion.

Knowing ourself, being ourself, and an environment where others will support us in knowing ourselves and being ourselves is not equivalent to the right to have others understand

and accommodate us. It is important to maintain ownership of our individual responsibility for and power over our sense of well-being. When disturbing ideas surround us and we choose our own emotional state, we have circular power. Also, space is created for diverse opinions to exist in the same room. People stay together and listen to each other long enough to explore for their areas of overlap.

Convincing others to do what we want is a disconnecting form of circular power. It asks them to ignore their internal guidance system in favour of our opinion. In circular thinking mode we know that ideas that make sense to people coming from several directions are robust and meaningful. Finding this area of overlap depends on people sharing their authentic views and never agreeing with something that they find to be flawed or unclear.

In linear thinking mode, optimal practice includes being able to convince people to accept our ideas. This can be confusing without a model for two ways of knowing. Linear operations include standards and job descriptions, and requirements for getting top grades. People shape their behaviour to match these requirements even if it sometimes doesn't make sense to them as individuals. This capitalizes on the increased ability to assert ones will when many are pulling in the same direction – as determined by the top of the hierarchy.

By contrast, circular leadership seeks to support others in knowing themselves and being themselves. This depends on the ability to read people through empathy, intuition, imagination, and authentic communication.

Chris Rufer imagined Morning Star Tomato Company to be an organization without managers or hierarchical structure. From this vision he created an organization that employs thousands of people at several tomato processing plants that supply ingredient tomato paste and diced tomato products to over 40% of the US markets.

The company's vision is that all team members will be "self-managing professionals, initiating communication and the co-ordination of their activities with fellow colleagues, customers, suppliers, and fellow industry participants; absent direction from others." As founder and CEO, Rufer's job is to support these behaviours.

If you were joining Morning Star, for example, after an orientation period, you'd write your personal mission statement for your tomato production task such as jarring a secret tomato recipe in an environmental and cost-conscious way. In consultation with the client, you would create a plan for doing that job. Getting the training, resources, and cooperation from other associates that you need to fulfill your mission would be your responsibility. You'd do this by reaching out to co-workers to enter into agreements known as "Colleague Letters of Understanding" to enlist support for completing your mission. Once these are in place you have the green light to do the job as you designed it.

In essence, Rufer is requiring his people to take responsibility for what makes their work meaningful. He is willing to empower them to make decisions from this foundation. In this operating system, workers are inspired by their mission and their commitments to each other. There is no need for managers.

At Morning Star, people listen to each other to understand what projects their colleagues are proposing and how they can help. With no competition to move up the job ladder, people are free to be supportive of each other. For example, if someone was purchasing a new piece of equipment, she would reach out to others to ensure the purchase meets the requirements of multiple users. When people have the freedom to work with you or not to work with you, cooperation happens naturally because being unreliable or undermining others' efforts kills your relational capital. It's like firing yourself.

Organically, relational capital became the major currency at Morning Star. As one employee put it, "All your energy goes into doing the best job you can do, and into helping your colleagues."

How does all of this translate into Morning Star's profit and loss statements? Having no middle managers saves as much as 33% of payroll and significantly increases employee engagement. The risk of making bad decisions decreases as the people directly involved in an issue have a say in the solutions. Rufer reports that his privately held company had double-digit annual profit growth from 1991 to 2011. The industry averaged 1% annual profit growth over the same period.

The Generative Principle

As mention previously, a by-product of the Goldilocks Test, which defines the positive and negative aspects of linear powers, is an affinity for averages. As we avoid the "too much" and "too little" options, we build a cluster of actions in the middle that get our attention and support. But sometimes, the most important part of the system is found in those rarer outliers.

Todd Rose, the author of *The End of Average* and director of the Mind, Brain, and Education program at Harvard, noticed how relying on averages can be detrimental.

At first, incorporating the concept of averages revolutionized some industries. Offering an average small, medium, and large clothing size, rather than customizing to each individual, for example, enabled mass production and reduced purchase costs. Tailors weren't very happy, but more people could suddenly afford many outfits. The clothing industry as a whole flourished.

Other areas did not do as well with the use of averages. In the 1940s, US Air Force fighter-plane cockpits needed to be designed in a way that maximized pilots' ability to rapidly take specific actions. The average body dimensions of hundreds of pilots were used in the design of the seating and controls placement. When planes started taking unintended dives, often resulting in fatalities, the engineers scrambled for an answer. Alas, they could find no mechanical or electrical problems.

By 1950, they wondered if pilots had changed in their dimensions. They produced a new set of average measurements based on ten key body traits of over 4,000 USAF pilots. It was during this exercise that a scientist noticed that not one of the pilots in the study was within 30% of the average of all ten of the body dimensions used to construct the cockpit. In other words, the assumption that averages are a good representation of individuals was fatally wrong.

With pilots dying at alarming rates, the US Air Force instructed the engineers to customize cockpits to individuals' body dimensions. At first the engineers resisted, saying it would be impossible and expensive. With insistence, the engineers stepped outside the linear thinking box and invented adjustable seats and straps. Travel of all kinds has since been made safer because of this ability to customize seats.

Education and medical treatments count on averages in a similar way. Jeffrey Rediger, the medical doctor, psychologist, and researcher we met earlier, looks at the rare phenomenon of spontaneous remission of "incurable" diseases in his book *Cured*. He found that medical research has been removing cases of spontaneous remission from studies, even when they are verifiable by medical evidence. These cases were disregarded because extreme outliers throw off the representation of the averages. As a result, the clues to finding cures offered by the high performers were sacrificed in favour of identifying the average outcomes.

Prescription drugs are dispensed based on the safe dosage

for the average person, and medical protocols in healthcare generally are based on the average outcomes of a population. Likewise, in school systems, schedules and grading processes are often designed to suit the non-existent average student. As Rose describes, "When you actually get the data, it (average-ism) rarely covers anyone."

When individuals matter, circular thinking can provide new opportunities for positive outcomes. Rather than reliance on data and norms, it trusts individual's and seeks ways to customize operations in response to their ability to identify their emotions and imagine their best lives.

Circular power has a qualifier that guides the positive and negative applications. I call it the Generative Principle which is:

> The emotion you give your attention to will grow
> and be contagious.

Said in a more circular way: whatever we choose to hold in our hearts will expand, in us and in others. In essence, we have the personal power in every moment to notice the array of emotions we are experiencing, and make a selection of which one we want to feed by giving it our attention.

Having agency over the emotions we give our attention to is a super power. We've all met the compulsive Eeyore-type who we try to give a wide birth in tough times. Imagine that guy pausing to self-reflect and finding feelings of disappointment, low self-confidence, and curiosity. With this awareness he can choose which of these emotions he wants to expand. Is it the right time to explore, spread, or perhaps outgrow feelings of disappointment and self-doubt? Or, is this the time to follow curiosity and creatively explore the issue at hand? This is what it looks like to own our internal world. When we claim our power over our thoughts, nobody can make us feel anything without our compliance. While multiple emotions continue to exist in our internal world, we are aware of our ability to turn the volume up or down on specific emotions by giving them our attention or setting them aside.

This circular thinking is in high contrast to linear power where we shut down all our emotions in favour of applying logic, reasoning, and rational thought.

With circular power, even suffering can become optional, as demonstrated by Viktor Frankl in his book *Man's Search for Meaning*. where he describes his experiences as a Jewish person in a Nazi concentration camp. Frankl found himself in a situation where he had no linear power to assert his will. His life was a living hell until one day he met a woman that made his heart flutter with new love. It seemed odd to him that in his fear-saturated environment this could happen. But there he was, occasionally swept up in feelings of love. Frankl realize that regardless of his external world, he had options in his internal world. He alone chose the feelings and beliefs that he would foster. When he chose to focus on love, he found moments of joy even in a horrific environment. No matter what his enemies did to him physically, they could not take away his freedom to select the emotions he would grow in his internal world.

In that moment where we pause, gain some internal awareness, and choose which emotion we will face the world through, we initiate states of personal insight, transformation, and an opportunity to be aspirational. We have circular power.

Essentially, the Generative Principle shows us the positive and negative sides of circular power. I got a big shock here. These positive and negative aspects are not good and bad designations, as they were in the linear world with its external focus. Awareness of our emotions shows us if we are in a state of connection (positive) or disconnection (negative) from our self. Awareness of both positive and negative love-based emotions is valuable for the insight it offers. Think of the positive and negative aspects of a photograph. Through awareness of the two halves of the whole we gain the power of knowing ourselves. Both positive and negative versions of love-based feelings are beneficial when we embrace and explore them. Reconnection and disconnection each have their time.

I liken it to playing a game of hot-and-cold. In this game, a person is searching for something they want. Players acting as Guides shout out messages in the form of a temperature gradient to indicate proximity to the prize. Shouts of "warm, warmer, hot" signal the Searcher is getting closer. Information like "cooler" alerts him or her to a move taking them away from the prize. In response to "cold!" the searcher completely changes direction until finding a warmer and eventually hot direction.

Notice how hot and cold signals are both good information. When we think about it, feelings of envy, loneliness, and isolation give us useful information about what we want more of. For example, envy points towards something we admire in a person. We could cultivate that quality in ourselves. Loneliness points to a desire for more connection. Disconnecting feelings of depression and self-doubt are cold signals to inspire more attention to our needs and capacity for growth. With conscious awareness of these shadow feelings, we have a direction to start exploring.

Feelings of disconnection can also highlight the need to set boundaries around what impacts us on a personal level. Behaviours like gossip, call-out culture, cancel-culture, gaslighting, ghosting, mobbing, and social media shaming are efforts to weaponize our emotions against us by fostering psychological disconnection from self. If we respond by moving away from the sources of disconnection, we create boundaries that keep these tactics from being effective. Instead, we move towards what connects us to our personal value. Our resilience is strengthened through our emotional awareness.

The final aspect of the Generative Principle is that our feelings are contagious. Scientific evidence of mirror neurons was first recognized in the early 1990s by a team of Italian neuroscientists at the University of Parma. In humans, these mirror neurons are the source of activities like imitation, decoding the meaning behind other people's actions, and fostering empathy. Humans have an uncanny ability to read the vocal tone, facial expressions, body language, and environmental cues of friends, family, co-workers. Highly empathic people can actually feel another's feelings as if they were their own.

Brain researcher and psychologist Daniel Siegel demonstrates the contagious nature of people's desires by gazing at a glass of water and then reaching for it and taking a drink. People watching report sudden feelings of thirst.

I cast my mind back to the elder drawing circles on the blackboard in northern Alberta and recognize that this is the power of the ever-expanding circles. When we want to be inclusive, for example, others want to satisfy that same desire and our circles grows. Likewise, these metaphorical circles shrink when someone is excluded.

Does this mean we are in danger of unconsciously adopting the emotional state of every person we are engaging with? This is a good question to ask ourselves. If so, the antidote is to consciously recognise what feelings we are experiencing and take responsibility for selecting the feeling that we will give our attention to. Making this internal choice reclaims our power.

In contrast to linear power, circular power does not try to shape other people's behaviour. Instead, we take responsibility for being our best self, including being caring, respectful, and curious. Other people may feel inspired to reflect and choose their own state of mind within this circular environment. This is a healthy form of contagion.

Daryl Davis, a Black jazz musician, was playing in the Silver

Dollar Lounge when, at the end of his set, he was invited to join a white, middle-aged man who had enjoyed his music. They got to talking about the origins of jazz. The white guy didn't believe that Jerry Lee Lewis was inspired by Black boogie-woogie and blues piano players. Davis responded by revealing he knew this because he was a friend of Jerry Lee Lewis. His new friend became even more disbelieving. They were laughing and enjoying the process of getting to know each other. As they clinked their glassed, the man sitting with Davis declared that he had never shared a drink with a Black man before. This time Davis was genuinely surprised. How was it that he had shared a beverage or a meal with thousands of white people, but that this man, at least 15 years older than him, was sharing his first drink with a Black man?

One evening, the man admitted that he was a member of the Ku Klux Klan. Nonetheless, he kept returning to hear Davis play, and they visited afterwards, developing their friendship. Eventually the man gave Davis his robes as a way of telling him that he had quit the Klan.

This is what happens with circular thinking. When we are in a trusting relationship, we open our hearts and learn more about ourselves through our engagement with others.

Davis decided to continue meeting Klansmen. Music and curiosity brought them together. He viewed Klan members as fellow human beings with a different perspective on the world.

In an interview, Davis said, "I decided to go around the country and sit down with Klan leaders and members to find out: How can you hate me when you don't even know me?"

He learned everything he could about the Klan perspective to support having good conversations. "As you build upon those commonalities, you're forming a relationship, and as you build that relationship, you're forming a friendship. That's what would happen. I didn't convert anybody. They saw the light and converted themselves," he said.

Our beliefs and ways of being are not fixed. According to Siegel, when our behaviours become dissident with our feelings, we experience great discomfort and develop a drive to bring them into alignment.

In *The Bridge* theory, through this internally driven process of positive psychology and circular power, we initiate our own transformations.

Governments, conventionally focused on civil order and services like roads, firefighting, or a land registry system, are increasingly also supporting citizen-driven initiatives. Research by the Community Foundations of Canada shows that seeding a sense of belonging by supporting community initiatives produces a cascade of side effects beyond the quantifiable. People feel healthier, both mentally and physically; their natural curiosity is inspired; they want to learn more, which supports personal engagement in their school, work, and political systems. In this way, connected people create emotionally and physically safer and more enjoyable neighbourhoods and workplaces. When people feel they can participate in the collective good, volunteerism, donations, and citizen participation in community activities all increase, along with resiliency in an emergency.

Similarly, the disconnecting feelings around issues like racism and sexism can be contagious when surrounded by like-minded people. When these ideas are exposed to the larger group, a great upheaval occurs. The linear instinct is to shut down the offending perspectives. Another option is to see an opportunity to explore something that was previously invisible and needs addressing in a circular way.

A woman who was in a relationship with Donald Sterling, owner of the LA Clippers basketball team, recorded their conversation and shared it on social media. In the recording Sterling said, "It bothers me a lot that you want to broadcast that you're associating with Black people." The NBA responded to the racism in this comment by decisively banning Sterling from the NBA for life and fining him $2.5 million. Many were impressed with the speed at which NBA commissioner Adam Silver addressed the issue by disassociating the league from Sterling and imposing a strong linear deterrent.

On an episode of *The Van Jones Show*, Sean Carter (Jay-Z) commented on how the NBA responded to this moment of racism and the opportunity that was missed. He said:

OK, that's one way to do it. Another way would have been to [let Sterling] have his team and let's talk about it together..., because once you do that [highly punitive actions], all of the other closet racists just run back in the hole.

You haven't fixed anything...You don't take the trash out, you keep spraying [perfume] over it to make it acceptable. As those things grow, you create a superbug...

Fear of consequences can bring short-term behavioural change, but as soon as the external source of fear is overcome, old behaviours return, sometimes with a vengeance. Invisible danger zones grow in secret places, or behind people's disguises.

Let's take a closer look at the contagious effect of disconnecting emotions. Starting from a place of connection (for example, to a limiting belief) we move next to disconnection as a vital step before finding reconnection (this time to a belief that better serves us today). As the underlying belief is being reconsidered in this process, compassion needs to be maintained for the people behind the negative ideas that come to the surface, even when what they have to say is hard to hear. It often surprises people that a period of revulsion, discomfort, or sense of loss, are necessary times of disconnection on the pathway to a group's growth and transformation.

In one of my workshops, we reached the mixer exercise where participants were asked to form small groups. I noticed Sarah, an Asian woman, was having trouble joining a group. I went over to be supportive and quickly understood that her intended partners, Betty and John, were not going to function smoothly with Sarah this weekend. I redirected and found Sarah a welcoming group.

In the first quiet moment I had, I stopped and thought about the interaction. Betty and John had given the lamest reasons that I had ever heard to not work with another person. I was triggered by every racially motivated hardship my children had experienced. My first impulse was to right a wrong.

I took a calming breath, and from the bridge perspective, I recognized I was in the fear-driven world, wanting justice, which was a radical departure from the purpose of the weekend workshop. I took a moment to consider what a shift to circular thinking would look like. Each of these participants was under my leadership care including Betty and John, and what makes me a good workshop facilitator is that I strive to offer all my participants an environment of kindness and respect. Every person showed up to my workshop willing to explore ideas, and I was grateful for that. Betty and John were triggered by something, just like I was, and their discomfort was resulting in a particular behaviour. I decided to give my attention to ensuring a welcoming environment for all – not just the ones that aligned with my comfort zone. With this mindset, the workshop grew to have a lovely atmosphere over the weekend. This is what circular power feels like. It is gentle, surprising, and impactful.

At the end of the workshop, Sarah came up to me and said, "Thank you for noticing my challenge and supporting me. This was a great experience." I was delighted to know that she had enjoyed the weekend. I marvelled that all I needed to do was check my own reactions to ensure that I was generating a receptive feeling towards everyone (a positive contagion). Humans are amazing in the ways we can read each other and match our responses.

As the crowd thinned, I noticed Betty waiting to talk to me. She looked pensive and said, "This was so unexpected. You did something here. It felt safe, even to explore...darker places. I'm not sure how you did it, but I'm impressed. Thank you. I feel energized, and peaceful." A smile transformed her face.

Now, I don't actually know if Betty was reflecting on the interaction I supported, or the workshop material, or something else. But if I harboured animosity towards her, she would not have enjoyed the workshop, nor had the potential for vulnerable reflection. (When we feel judged, we become fixed and defensive.) Even Sarah would have felt the tension if I had subtly expressed disapproval toward Betty and John over the weekend.

This workshop experience confirmed my theory that we cannot impose change on another person and shouldn't try because it risks generating the opposite effect. What we can do, however, is create a place of respectful inclusion that seeds the best possible outcomes.

Hearing perspectives that are offensive to us is not a comfortable place to hang out, but if we remain engaged, the discomfort leads to important insights that catalyze change. Circular leaders know to hold a space for growth to occur.

There are times when people are not ready to grow through their stuck places. It's just not the right moment. In these times, we can put the issue on hold while we choose to give our attention to other thoughts and feelings.

A First Nation man once told me that in his community, they talk about the hook at the door where people hang all their grudges and bad feelings before joining the meeting. It's a great image. It creates a moment to pause and reflect on our inner world, to notice what needs to go on the hook, and enter with our receptive emotions. This access to our circular power of knowing ourselves and choosing what emotions we will feed allows us to take ownership of what we bring to the discussion.

Disconnection and Reconnection

Let's take a closer look at this concept of disconnection and reconnection. As previously mentioned, when our attention is placed on our internal world, we find an array of emotions. The fear-based emotions send us into linear thinking, where we promptly get our emotions under control. Meanwhile, our love-based emotions open up all the processes of circular thinking. We become aware of our love-based emotions and the power to choose which one or ones to grow. These emotions are related to some form of connectedness including disconnection (which are sometimes necessary), a longing for reconnection, or a desire to expand our places of existing connection.

The circular world is not a zero-sum game. It is a generative system where our various states of connectedness can be expanded in limitless ways. The Generative Principle highlights our power over the nature of those expansions.

The impulse to disconnect from harmful relationships causes us to separate, wander in the wilderness, and consider new possibilities for reconnection. Feelings of indifference, distraction, recklessness, craving, and numbness are also messages that we are in this state of disconnection. The question becomes why? There may be a limiting belief that once served us and is now working against us from the inside. We can choose if we want to continue to spiral downward creating disconnection or find reconnection. States such as self-doubt, depression, self-sabotage, and anxiety can separate us from our awareness of our intrinsic worthiness of belonging and respect. They can also initiate an exploration of our limiting beliefs and seed change.

Similarly, we may be storing memories of experiences we no longer have access to, perhaps because someone died. The sorrow from this disconnect can be a precursor to joy, and a sense of what's meaningful, as Susan Cain explores in her book *Bittersweet: How Sorrow and Longing Make Us Whole*. Cain reminds us that the places where we feel hurt mark the things we care about. It may seem easier to keep the memory alive by hanging onto the heartache, but paying attention to our sorrow allows us to emerge with a heart able to know joy.

Emotions like resonance, engagement, authenticity, enjoyment, happiness, purpose, and passion are all indications of connection to our talents, highest sense of self, and positive beliefs. It is through choice that we follow these open-heartedly.

I recall a time when I appreciated the opportunity to learn how to shift disconnection to reconnection from Yukon First Nations ways of knowing. I was a land negotiator on the Federal Government's team. By the time I joined the Yukon First Nation Comprehensive Land Claim Negotiations, the Federal and Yukon governments and the Yukon First Nations had been talking to each other to resolve land claim issues for over 20 years. One day I showed up to work and learned Ottawa had told us that if we didn't show significant progress, and very soon, our funding would be shifted to another region.

Lawyers and senior representatives of the three parties sat at main-table negotiations. The Federal team was definitely in a fear-based environment. Even the Yukon government needed this agreement to be completed or they would face an unhappy electorate in the upcoming election. Thorny issues such as limits on self-government powers and finalization of land parcels had the First Nations on edge as well.

The Federal negotiators had just pitched a solution that was difficult for the First Nations to hear, and an elder responded by speaking of the devastating effect of the residential school program, where hundreds of children were shamed, and neglected, sometimes resulting in death. He pleaded for his people's need to get back to the land to heal.

Several government representatives at the meeting were moved to the edge of tears. Others just stared at the table in front of them, frustrated that the talks had become so emotional. It felt unjust to them that they were being blamed for past actions that they had no part in and no ability to fix. Meanwhile, they were losing valuable time.

No one knew what to do. We sat in silence, way beyond a white man's comfort zone.

Finally, the First Nations' chief negotiator, Dave Joe, pulled out his cell phone. He flipped it open (state of the art at the time), and spoke into it saying, "Beam me up, Scottie. It is REALLY tough down here."

Everyone stared at him in shocked silence. Then we all burst into laughter, recognizing our shared experience with the *Star Trek* crew in a cross-cultural jam. Dave chuckled like a mischievous boy, probably a lot like he did in those residential school days in the precious moments when he played hockey with his friends. A welcome sense of relief filled the room. We were in this moment, together, laughing (a deeply human act).

Then Dave looked around the circle from person to person, and, as I recall, said, "When I look around this table, I see good and smart people who are all working on these very hard issues. This is very tough for all of us. After 20-some years of negotiation, we are nearing the end. This is not the 'somewhat interesting pile.' This is the 'too hard' pile we are tackling now. And the path to get here has been painful. But a lot of hard work, from all sides, has gotten us very close to completing an agreement. Ultimately, we are here because we all want to be a part of a better future for us Indians. Let's put our minds together and see what we can do."

And we did.

Dave Joe knew the circular power of humour to reconnect us to each other. He didn't use sarcastic humour, or even intellectual humour that only the insiders would get. It was an "Isn't life grand!" kind of humour that everyone could embrace and feel nourished by. Then he validated what everyone was feeling, and valued each person's contribution. In short, he restored everyone's sense of being emotionally connected and appreciated.

The Generative Principle has a big impact on our states of disconnection and reconnection. In a state of disconnection in interpersonal relationships, for example, we generate more disconnection. If we choose to pause and shift to reconnection, we reverse the trend. Likewise, shifting an organization's culture requires awareness of this moment of choice.

Today, workers want to see their values reflected in the companies they work for. Millennials in particular are well known for wanting to align their work with the things they care about. They want their work and their values to be connected.

Google workers began a movement to have some influence over the projects that their talents were serving. This contributed to Google's decision to abandon Project Maven, a lucrative contract with the Pentagon creating software for targeted drone strikes. The Google workers wanted their intellectual abilities to positively contribute to society. Similarly, workers at Apple and Facebook (Meta Platforms) have called on companies to change how they work. These initiatives from the inside of companies may be a crucial companion to the external efforts of regulators for creating a safe internet society.

Connection to shared values is gaining the importance that was once reserved for the potential for economic gains. Shoppers want to be able to feel good about their purchases and investors want to know they are also contributing to the well-being of people and the planet. Over the last decade, companies have increasingly made this value part of their brand. For example, responsible sourcing of battery raw materials is a focus for Tesla. The company now enters into direct contracts with mines to ensure that the metals in their car batteries are mined in a humane and eco-sensitive way. Talon Metals Tamarack Nickel-Copper-Cobalt Project recently entered into a contract with Tesla that includes the use of technology to suck carbon dioxide out of the atmosphere and bind it to rocks in the mine, making their nickel production carbon neutral.

Responsible Steel is an international multi-stakeholder membership organization that offers certification to ensure buyers that their materials are sourced and produced with consideration for clean water, carbon footprint reduction, positive governance, and respectful local involvement. The member companies hold a vision of being contributors to a sustainable society.

Just as the tide goes in and out, the moon waxes and wanes, connection and disconnection each have their time.

Chapter 5
The Bridge

There is a pattern to human thought processes. The power of this insight is in the hands of the person who recognizes it.

Taking possession of this pattern holds the key to a new foundational understanding of areas like how to address climate change, conduct successful and meaningful businesses, resolve conflicts, and nurture individual happiness. These initiatives require conscious application of our full human capacity, namely linear and circular thinking. Currently we are successfully activating systems that support one half of that potential.

The bridge framework separates linear and circular thinking states to reveal a simple yet profound pattern: namely, three core operating principles that provide an entryway into each of these thinking styles.

Here's a scenario that describes the large-scale pattern of linear thinking:

An external danger activates a fear response, and the portal to linear thinking opens; we enter a world where one or all of these three principles govern our thinking:

1. we objectively focus on the external world;
2. we push back against potential causes of physical pain or external threats to our goals, and

3. we evaluate life through an "either this or that, but not both" lens (either/or).

On the other half of our pattern of thinking there is a portal to circular thinking with a scenario that goes like this:

A heart or gut impulse is activated, pulling up associated beliefs, and emotion laden memories in our interior world. We walk through the doorway to circular thinking where we:

1. give attention to our internal world and subjective feelings;
2. pull in what compels us to make a connection or disconnection, and
3. say, "Yes, I can relate to what is being offered, and here is something to add. Let's find ways for these ideas to co-exist" (yes-and-both).

We are all capable of our own version of linear and circular thinking, but their operating systems are often invisible to us. The concept of two ways of knowing provides a means for sorting linear from circular thinking to reveal their unique internal designs. The first thing to notice is that they are opposite in nature. The bridge framework is a tool for connecting them by providing the criteria for first separating circular from linear thinking. With conscious awareness of the operating differences, we have a bridge to move from one to the other with intention.

Trying to do a linear task with circular methods is like facing a charging grizzly bear and asking yourself, "What makes this situation meaningful?" Instead, we need to respect the fear, get control over our emotions, and make some either/or decision. Freeze or run?

Equally, going on a first date and leaning across the table to whisper, "I'd like to see some measurable progress in our relationship in the next hour," is clearly an inappropriate application of linear thinking.

When we find ourselves unsure of how to proceed in situations more subtle than the examples above, we can stand on the neutral deck of the bridge and ask ourselves some questions like this one: Am I pushing back against what is being suggested?

If the answer is yes, I'm in a linear mindset (push-back). It might help to know that all the other operating principles of linear thinking have also been activated, including an emotional base of fear. Is there a physical danger I need to push back against? If not, this may be a situation best handled from a circular perspective. What if I were to cross the bridge to circular thinking, just for a moment. I do this by being receptive to what is being suggested, which is a form of pulling in with imagination to consider ways in which this new idea might be beneficial.

Here's another question: Am I thinking this is an either/ or decision?

Then I am in my linear mindset. Is there a definitive right or wrong, better or worse solution to this problem? If not, I can expand the options by taking a yes-and-both approach. To do this I might say "yes, I agree with this part, and I could add to it in this way."

These types of questions support us in pausing between two potentials to see and consider both options. The pause and the sorting create the bridge.

I first saw Anne Giardini as chancellor of Simon Fraser University, when she was about to make a speech. I knew of her impressive work as past president of Weyerhaeuser Company, a large forestry operation, but I had yet to meet her.

A petite woman in a lemon-yellow summer dress that complemented her soft brown eyes walked onto the stage. With a smile, she said, "Not what you expected?"

Giardini's speech focused on an experience she had when negotiating with the Haida Nation on BC's northern coast. That experience had not been what she expected either. She began by saying, "First, be aware you know less than you think you know. Challenge your own assumptions."

She went on to describe a conversation she had with a Haida leader when Weyerhaeuser leaders travelled to the community to secure support for a project. Giardini shared, "The Chief said, 'You assume we want a wage economy.' He was right. I did assume that. Who doesn't want to get paid? He didn't."

Giardini's story about assuming everyone in the conversation is thinking like us teaches a great lesson. Weyerhaeuser was being progress-driven and transactional, following principles that characterize Western businesses. These are also hallmarks of linear thinking. The Haida leader was showing her that not everyone is coming from the same worldview. I would describe this willingness to explain and make a connection as a form of circular thinking.

The bridge doesn't tell us what to think, or what someone else is thinking. It gives us the latticework to hang our ideas on in an environment that supports understanding.

Choosing to employ one or more of the operating principles of either linear or circular thinking is like flipping a switch that suddenly activates the entirety of that thinking mode. This is a powerful thing.

At first it is awkward to apply the bridge, but eventually we'll move naturally from one world to the other without even thinking about how we did it.

Here is a snapshot of the bridge structure we are exploring in this book:

LINEAR THINKING: Assert your will even against resistance	CIRCULAR THINKING: Know yourself, be yourself, and support others in doing the same
1. External	1. Internal
2. Push-back	2. Pull-in
3. Either/Or	3. Yes-And-Both

The linear operating systems we are about to explore will be familiar to Western readers, possibly so ever-present that their basic nature is invisible. The juxtaposition of the linear with its circular counterparts illuminates the nature of the gap between these two ways of knowing, and offers a bridge.

Linear Operating Principle 1: External Lens

Linear mode always has its eye on the outside world. Perhaps this is because the danger-alerting information we're interested in is found out there. Fear is the appropriate response to impending physical hardship. When activated, it gives us a helpful early warning system, while there is still time to shape our best outcome through our actions.

Objective
Information from the external world is coming to us as facts. From it we draw logical conclusions. Therefore, an external focus naturally leads to high value being placed on the objective. After a fear-based emotion signals the presence of a danger, we control our feelings to prevent contamination of the information. Paying attention to feelings may lead to overreactions and short-sighted decisions, or cause us to stand frozen like a deer in car headlights. Staying cool and level-headed while taking measured action under pressure is

the mark of a professional. Linear thinking, with its external focus, is therefore inherently objective.

The word "objective" is synonymous with a goal that is specific and measurable in the external world. It can also be a state of mind, free of bias, favoritism, or other emotional influences. An objective frame of mind is what makes the scientific method so reliable, for example. Any person, at any time, will be able to reproduce the same result, if they accurately follow the method.

Objectivity also protects us from being distracted by other people's feelings. Being overly concerned about the emotional impact of our actions on our opponent, for example, severely reduces our competitive edge.

The movie *A League of Their Own,* captures this message. This film is about the women's baseball league that started during World War II. In it, Tom Hanks plays the coach who gives one of his players his opinion on her lousy technique. The player bursts into tears, and the coach is truly affronted.

"Are you crying?" he exclaims. "There's no crying in baseball!"

In linear thinking, goal achievement outweighs hurt feelings most of the time. The exception is when we consider the level of retaliation that might result as a consequence of hurt feelings.

Conventional management practices are set up to support objectivity. Budgets, risk assessments, and policies all limit human variability and drama. Laws, rules, procedures, and contracts provide consequences for non-compliance. They are applied uniformly in the name of fairness, and on the basis of facts rather than an individual's story. Deadlines are also to be met without consideration of personal feelings (aka excuses). If a person falls behind, they are expected to stoically dig down, stay focused, and work longer and harder to get back on track with the plan.

Goals and Direction

Goals define the end point of something we want to achieve in the external world. The best goals are measurable and specific. Saying, "We want to do a better job of getting our message out there," is not specific enough to be a goal. "Our goal is to increase the number of views on our website by 20% by the end of this fiscal year" is a goal.

At the 50th anniversary of the first lunar landing, journalist Joel Achenbach noted, "Though everything about the moonshot was fraught with uncertainty, it benefited from a clearly defined goal. In May 1961, President John F. Kennedy asked NASA to put a man on the moon and bring him safely back to Earth before the decade was out." Another aspect of NASA's goal was to land on the moon prior to the Russians. This competition was a major driving force in the space program.

Effort has a clear direction when a goal is well-defined with a limited scope. We can strategize the necessary steps, ensure every step is properly resourced, and track our progress towards the goal because we know what the final product has to look like. We also know when we are done and if we failed or achieved our goal. The goal and its action plan become a visual representation of our linear efforts to assert our will, even against resistance.

Planning tools like budgets, management flow charts, or architectural drawings can actualize the goal when it is well-defined. Actions not in line with our plan can be set aside to ensure they are not a waste of our limited resources.

It is also worth noting that nothing in the US goal to stand on the moon spoke to moon-life after being first. As a result, after July 20, 1969, when the US won the race, there was no structural basis for a long-term presence in space. With a focus on the record of who won the race to the moon, the mission design did not include precursors to putting a space station on the moon, for example. As a result, most of the products of this space program were not usable for anything else.

Goal setting takes advantage of the benefits of a hierarchy, provides clarity of direction, and efficiently manages resources. It supports groups of people in channeling their efforts to achieve more than is individually possible.

Measurability

In this externally focused, goal-setting world, what's measured is what matters.

Data is appreciated for its objective reliability as it moves from person to person. Metrics are popular tools because they track progress and productivity through trustworthy data, free of human bias. Furthermore, the knowledge we gain from measurability can be relied on from decade to decade by virtue of its being objectively recorded. In this way, each generation can stand on the shoulders of the understandings and inventions of its predecessors.

Also, the data can be analysed to produce a trend-lines from the past to the present. If we assume a measure of consistency, this provides a predictor of the future. The resulting lead-time gives us the ability to capitalize on the trend. Or we can attempt to influence the controlling parameters and bend the trend.

Measurability was a powerful attention getter in the 2006 documentary *An Inconvenient Truth* which graphically depicted the environmental trend we were on. Car-driving, hamburger-eating, consumer-driven cultures paused in their tracks to watch the film. Based on data, it pictorially described what will happen if the ice caps continue to melt and sea level rises all around the world; it showed how millions of people will be flooded from coastal cities, droughts will lead to starvation, while elsewhere hurricanes will leave a wake of destruction. Former US Vice President Al Gore's statement that US and China fossil fuel consumption was emitting carbon dioxide equivalent to 400,000 Hiroshima bombs a day was scary stuff. Gore had made the problem measurable. It was a strong call to action.

Making things measurable can also help us control our emotions and achieve objectivity. Imagine bobbing in a boat on the ocean when the crackling radio announces that there is a storm coming. Our imagination starts to work overtime, and we are potentially facing *The Perfect Storm*. On the other hand, if we hear there is a storm coming with winds of 35 knots, we can compare this information to the challenges we have faced in the past. This allows thoughts like, "I have navigated winds of 32 knots before. This is beyond my experience but most likely within my capacity." In this way, measurements provide a tool for getting emotions under control and pave the way for logical and rational thinking.

Since measurability offers all these benefits, soon what is measured becomes the only thing that matters. This can prove to be detrimental when a situation is impacted by human psychology.

The UN Climate Change talks aspire to global behavioral transformation to prevent and rehabilitate detrimental climate changes from human impacts. They believe that billions of people, with varying degrees of free will and motivation, can undergo a massive shift in behaviour. The UN first established these Climate Change gatherings in 1995 when the global community started to sense that glaciers were melting, deserts were expanding, and flooding and hurricanes were occurring in unprecedented places.

The set-up for the *Conference of the Parties to the UN Convention on climate change (COP)* gives the host country the ability to design the meeting, within a few UN guidelines. The most significant of these guidelines is the requirement for a final consensus vote among the member nations to affirm resolutions from the meeting. This principle of inclusivity makes circular dynamics necessary for a significant part of UN Climate Change talks.

The popularity of Al Gore's *An Inconvenient Truth* was a catalyst for heightened global interest in climate change going into COP 15 in 2009. With fear levels rising among all the approximately 195 UN member countries, as well as global citizens, Copenhagen prepared for the fifteenth Climate Change Conference.

As would be expected in a fear-driven environment, many linear tactics were employed in these talks. People saw themselves as separate from others and were grasping for linear power. Upon arrival in Copenhagen, participants learned of a "leaked" document that the host government had secretly penned, in consultation with a select group of countries. Presumably this agreement would be ready to introduce if progress towards the goal of a binding commitment to limit global temperature increase to 2 degrees Celsius was slow. Progress was being placed ahead of inclusion of all countries' perspectives.

In the opening remarks, the Danish Prime Minister, Lars Rasmussen made statements like, "... "I realize that as the host, I ought not to rush things, but rather encourage you all to get comfortable, before we embark on the daunting task before us. Unfortunately, we do not have the time for such courtesy and protocol," and "The grim projections from science grow more alarming each day.... The coming days will offer ample risks of being blind-sided by animosity, difficulty, complexity, or downright fear." These statements pushed relationship development to the background in favour of motivation to progress towards a specific goal through warnings of the dangers to expect.

The host failed to recognize that countries attending the

Copenhagen talks had a shared problem, but not a shared goal. A shared problem is when several people are affected by a situation, but they may be affected in different ways and hold very different requirements for the resolution. A shared goal has group commitment to a specific outcome and acknowledgement that it is best achieved by the development of a hierarchy, allowing efforts to be effectively co-ordinated in the agreed upon direction. As it was, with people having different agendas within an objective linear mindset, a pushing match developed.

In this goal dominated environment, there was lots of talking, but it was unclear if people were really listening. According to Edward Snowden, the US bugged some private caucus areas to gain a competitive advantage. The Copenhagen diplomats noted that the US as well as the China teams were suspiciously well informed. There were also accusations of UK spying. Extracting information, rather than engaging with people, is a very objective form of listening and a classic example of using linear techniques to be expedient.

A sense of distrust pervaded the talks. Participants regularly stormed out of negotiations and expressed discouragement to the press as they recounted how the talks failed to be inclusive or transparent.

Frustrated with the lack of progress, US President Obama hashed out an agreement with South Africa, India, China, and Brazil. In the final vote there was no consensus and the agreement was "taken note of" but not formally passed by the assembled nations.

Objectively using linear power to address climate change was thwarted by the circular elements of the gathering.

Loyalty

The organizational system for a goal-driven scenario is a hierarchy with the leader at the top responsible for establishing the overall goal for the team. Fear drives progress – fears like falling behind our competitors, letting the team down, equipment failure, wasting limited resources, or missing a deadline. This mindset gives us the motivation to work against what might go wrong. We know what the objective is and we fulfill our role to be a positive member of the team.

Enemies know that if the leader of a hierarchy is disabled, it throws the organization into chaos. To protect against this weakness caused by external forces, the teams offer their loyalty in the form of action and words of allegiance to those above them in the chain of command when facing the outside world. Hesitation can be costly. Being able to rely on a large and rapid protective response increases a team's chances of survival and success. Loyalty protects the power centre.

Loyalty can also take the form of endurance. No matter how many obstacles, distractions, or the steepness of the climb, we keep working hard and making progress towards the goal out of loyalty to the group. Sacrifices are made and short-term pain is accepted in favour of the potential benefits of team success.

Another strong incentive for demonstrating one's loyalty is increased likelihood of being promoted up the hierarchical chain.

As with all linear operating systems, the Goldilocks Test needs to be activated to ensure proper use of loyalty.

In response to a substantial increase in the number of failed attempts to get access to information, especially from the premier's office, Elizabeth Denham, as the BC Information and Privacy Commissioner, conducted an investigation. She released a report entitled *Access Denied: Record Retention and Disposal Practices of the Government of British Columbia.*

In Denham's investigation of BC Government practices in response to access to information applications, an incident was discovered where records had been destroyed in response to an information request.

The investigation found that Tim Duncan of the BC Transportation and Infrastructure Ministry received an access to information request regarding Highway 16 – the infamous Highway of Tears in northern BC. Duncan located between 12 and 20 related emails in his mailbox and showed them to his supervisor, George Gretes. Duncan testified that Gretes then triple-deleted the emails from Duncan's computer. Despite Gretes' denial, Commissioner Denham found Duncan to be a reliable witness.

In terms of expressing loyalty, blocking access to documents that could bring government under unfavourable scrutiny was a loyal move. Arguably it failed to pass the Goldilocks Test because it negatively impacted the democratic principle behind a law. There is such a thing as "too much" loyalty.

Preserve and Protect

Concern over threats to our people, property, or perspectives motivates the development of tools like written rights and policies, safety practices, and maintenance procedures. If we don't defend and maintain our resources and achievements, they will be constantly eroding.

In warfare, history has shown that people are far more likely to surrender to an enemy that they believe to be fair and honourable. In George Washington's day, every soldier in the Continental Army signed a set of rules designed to protect civilians. Soldiers committed to respecting "the rights of humanity" and to taking restrained actions that will "justly secure to us the attachment of all good men."

Many countries have signed the Geneva Convention,

which has similar intent. It states that all wounded and sick are to be collected and cared for with the best available medical care by the party with the power to provide it.

During active combat, US soldiers have been known to transport a wounded enemy sniper to receive medical attention even though that sniper just killed their buddy. Doctors provide care to the sniper, often using blood donations from what they call the "walking blood bank" of soldiers. Once stable, the sniper is returned to his people for recovery.

These are not decisions that are easily made in the heat of the moment. Imagine what goes through the head of the nurse who sits alone with that sniper in the helicopter during transport. The thing preventing him from taking revenge is his self-control and the oaths and protocols established when rational thought determined the best plan for preserving and protecting the country's honor. The strategy is to take actions that earn the respect rather than the righteous indignation of their enemy and protect the integrity of their cause.

In the Golan Heights hundreds of wounded Syrians have been known to sit by the fence along the Israel-Syrian front, waiting to be found by Israeli soldiers on night patrol. They trust that they will be given good medical treatment. Citizens have commented on how their understanding of the enemy changed after friends and family received this kind of ethical care.

Requirements for honourable behaviour during wartime is a powerful example of how asserting our will over our emotions can preserve and protect the broader values of a group.

An external focus leads to objectivity, development of goals, high value placed on measurability, expressions of loyalty, and a drive to preserve and protect our gains. These have become gold standards in many of our societal structures.

Circular Operating Principle 1: Internal Lens

The first operating principle of circular thinking, an internal lens is our structural base. Here, we access circular power through self-reflection, gut instinct, and heart-felt intuition. We trust this self-knowledge as we take action in the world. It's all very subjective. Through reflection we find our sources of creativity, wisdom, and common sense. Conflict resolution, deep work engagement, resilience, and a culture of belonging all become possible. We also find our triggers, limiting beliefs and the transformative power of circular thinking to observe, explore and release them. This is not always a comfortable ride.

Subjective

Linear thinking is like being a train on a track. With our engine in well maintained order, we set out towards the next station. Every obstacle we encounter must be addressed and overcome. When the terrain gets steeper, we dig down and work harder. Our job is to safely arrive at the destination on time.

Circular thinking is a walk on the beach with the smell of a fresh breeze and the sound of lapping waves. As we offerings from the sea we pick up a rock or a seaweed that attracts our attention and examine it from different angles. Our pockets begin to fill up with beautiful shells. As we turn back towards home, we start letting go some of our treasures, keeping only the most evocative of the joy of this walk on the beach. We look up and we are back where we started, richer for the experience of communing with nature.

An internal, subjective focus results in paying attention to the moment rather than setting an intention and marking progress towards that predetermined outcome.

Brian, an exploration company CEO and engineer, had a drilling project that was in jeopardy "because a bureaucrat had failed to do his job," as he described it. Brian felt righteously indignant because he had submitted the required regulatory paperwork months beforehand. Now he needed the First Nation land officer, Nancy, to sign off within the next few days on the licence application that she had just received. Otherwise, Brian would have had to pay drillers to sit around waiting for the go-ahead, while snow began to fall. This kind of delay would have cost the company a lot of money, as well as credibility with its shareholders.

On the other side of this battle of wills, the law provides the First Nation with 30 days to respond after receipt of an application. Brian's stress levels were understandably high. He was intensely driven to achieve his goal and there were significant barriers.

Brian's word choices and body language revealed his plan to assert his will to make progress even against resistance. In this moment Nancy was his obstacle. Brian had an upcoming meeting with her where he planned to proclaim the unfairness of the process and encourage her to sign off, forthwith.

The last thing Nancy wanted was to make a hasty decision in response to industry pressure. If I were her, faced with Brian's aggressive attitude, I might have taken my sweet 30 days to respond. That is the linear response: when pushed – push back harder.

I received a call from Brian asking for advice. Given his low levels of linear power in this situation, I suggested he try a circular approach. Humanize the meeting, rather than focus on making progress. When Nancy began to feel comfortable with Brian as a person, they could perhaps develop some trust between them.

"I could do that," Brian said. "I'll start slow. Ask where she's coming from on this application."

"That is less aggressive, but still pressuring Nancy to make linear progress on the application," I said. "I'm suggesting you try a completely different approach. Share something of yourself and take an interest in what she wants to share about herself. No agenda. Simply find something you have in common."

An hour later, the phone rang.

"I just got out of the meeting. I'm feeling a bit conflicted," Brian said with a chuckle. "I was expected to be saying it didn't work but it was amazing. I can hardly believe it. "I'd seen her at a fundraiser last night, so we talked about that. No other plan."

"That sounds like a good start."

"It really surprised me. When I was not trying to make progress, it was so much easier to listen. Without an agenda, I could actually hear what she was saying. It was startling. I suddenly realized that I'm always thinking about what I will counter with, or only hearing the parts that are in line with where I want the conversation to go. It was quite something how different this was."

"What a great insight," I said.

"Then it got even better. In the last 15 minutes of our time, out of the blue, Nancy told me that she didn't understand a couple of parts of my application. I had almost forgotten about the application," Brian said with a chuckle. "It was easy to explain what was being proposed. And I really wanted to help her get a clear idea of what we would be doing. Nancy didn't have any issues with what we proposed and offered to get a response out later that afternoon. I was so surprised. I made more progress not trying to make progress."

Even in a pressure cooker fear-driven situation, Brian was able to cut his lifeline to linear thinking because he could imagine another approach. The elation in his voice was wonderful.

In a linear pushing match, Nancy would be hesitant to

admit that she didn't understand part of the application – that would read as a weakness. However, when Brian opened the door to the subjective world of circular thinking, vulnerability was re-envisioned as a doorway to mutual understanding. As Brian switched his mindset from linear to circular thinking, he showed interest in building trust on a human level. Nancy naturally followed suit and was able to ask a question of the person most qualified to give a full answer. This is the beauty of the Generative Principle: you generate more of whatever you offer from your heart, and it is contagious.

Circular leadership cultivates the art of open listening by staying in the moment. From this position we can read what is happening around us from another person's perspective. This is far more difficult than it may sound, but when we do it, people willingly start to share what is important to them.

What if it had gone the other way, and Nancy had a substantive problem with the application? If Brian had stayed in circular mode, he would have been in the best possible position to really understand the nature of the problem. They might have been able to work jointly to find a solution that met both their interests. As an added bonus, when the next unpredicted snag unfolded, one of them would pick up the phone as soon as the problem arose, or calm people down with reassurance that the company will listen. In short, they would have more resilience and ability to face the next problem together.

On the other hand, if the problem was not resolvable, it would have been better for Brian to know that and look around for the next best property to invest in, rather than engaging in a pushing match for the life of the project. As an added bonus, respecting the Indigenous people's wishes would have also earned Brian and his company a reputation for being trustworthy and truly collaborative as he goes into his next project.

Subjectivity is an excellent guide whenever stepping into the unknown where things are not predictable.

Some people hear this story and see a trick for achieving their goals. Why not pretend to be personally interested, with the hopes that their opponent will be soft on them? However, circular power is founded on authenticity and can't be gamed like this for long. It is what is in your heart that is understood by the listener. Eventually circular thinkers recognize insincerity and the resulting disillusionment is long-lasting.

"Soft power" is a term coined by Joseph S. Nye Jr., of Harvard University. He defines it as "the ability to affect others to obtain the outcomes one wants through attraction rather than coercion or payment." In short, it is a manipulation of people's emotions.

Nye recognizes three forms of international diplomacy's power to gain support for a country's goals: payments (the proverbial carrot), threats (sticks), and the power of story to get people to want what another country wants through the perception that a country's culture or economy is highly desirable (soft power). This kind of story goes something like this: if they like our art, baseball, comics, or music, they will accept our foreign policy. This capitalizes on the human tendency to want to be in alignment with people we admire.

Soft power seeks to introduce a cool factor to unconsciously create acceptance of a country's diplomatic efforts through several forms including persuasion, charisma, and propaganda. At its best it can be an effective alternative to hard power such as war.

On a cautionary note, soft power activates love-based feelings and converts them into a linear advantage. The recipient needs to recognize this in order to avoid trickery. This is a place where the bridge framework can be very useful for sorting out what is happening on a communications level.

Soft power is not to be confused with positive circular power, which also engages people through arts and culture, but with the intent to connect on a human level. Circular relationships support and celebrate people's unique qualities such as Japan's anime style of art and US's baseball. Relationships based on appreciation of uniqueness foster the impulse to reach towards each other while maintaining our individuality.

Evelyn Fox Keller, a theoretical physicist, mathematical biologist, feminist philosopher, historian of science (and a person whose curiosity seems to know no bounds) noticed that science values objectivity, typically categorized as masculine and, by default, devalues subjectivity, which is typically categorized as feminine. In her book *Reflections on Gender and Science*, she noted how women scientists often respond to this objectivity/subjectivity messaging by hiding their gender. To combat the assumption that lacking a male gender made them prone to being "emotional" and less suitable for valuable scientific contributions, women sometimes use their initial and last name. For example, I might write myself as "K. E. Hudson" to hide my gender and make myself more suitable for publication.

Hiding our feminine names inadvertently supports the concept that science must be done through an objective lens. Keller states, "Why is it that we don't talk about the subjective and emotional aspects of doing science? It's not by chance. It's a matter of values."

This brings up an important question. How often are circular processes dismissed because they seem like an inappropriate response through an objective linear filter?

For circular thinkers, shutting down our emotions, as required for linear, logical thought, removes access to the fascinating nuances, insights, and wisdoms our human abilities allow us. This is why circular thinkers find it difficult to accept an environment that ignores emotions. It renders them powerless.

This is often the source of a clash between linear and circular thinkers. When circular thinkers are asked to explain their approach or their values, they often face a system that requires them to do this within the constructs of linear thinking – without the use of their emotional perceptions.

Many oral cultures face this dilemma. During Colin O'Neil's research, he walked into a room where First Nation workers were reflecting on the challenges of operating their government within a Euro-Canadian governance framework. They described the feeling of facing this cross-cultural clash well with the following statement:

What do you do? Like, what are you supposed to do? And constantly, while you're doing all of this, you have to participate in this process with, you know, ten per-cent of the level of human capacity that the other gov-ernments have and your work is tripled because you're also trying to educate them as you go along. And you're trying to educate people who are so closed to the idea that there's even another way of doing things. It's just, it's such an uphill...

Intriguingly, as the speaker struggles to find words that describe the nature of the underlying problem, he or she is providing a great example of what circular thinking looks like. As participants step into the unknown, there will be uncom-fortable endeavours to find words that capture the nature of the issues, often discarding one word but grateful for how it leads to another. Sharing gut feelings and heart-felt intuition are part of the self-possession it takes to be authentic and vulnerable on the journey to find wisdom. These emotional expressions, moving with the flow of feelings, offer an energy for others to connect to and add onto. In this emotion-cen-tred environment, people strive to develop clear language for sharing core concepts, and open avenues for further curiosity. It is a process that often reveals robust new concepts.

Linear thinkers' fear of wasting time often impels them to shut down this subjectivity because it looks like haphazard floundering. With an understanding of two ways of knowing, we can recognize that moving with the guidance of our points of discomfort is integral to circular thinking.

As an aside, fewer staff is a detriment to working in linear systems and an asset to working in circular systems where all departments can meet and be heard.

Linear processes need to be put on pause for circular processes to happen, otherwise conversation shrivel under the scrutiny for facts, progress, and focus.

Resilience is fostered in an organization that creates processes for exploring feelings. In a small government department, a letter arrived from a First Nation expressing anger that they had not been consulted properly on an activity in their traditional territory. The director of the department, Dian, brought everyone into the boardroom to share how she was feeling and check in with others. Several people felt hurt because they had sincerely tried to do the right thing. Others were confused as to what is expected of them. They sat with that for a minute as they sipped warm cups of tea.

Dian then told her people how she appreciated them for sharing how they felt and for the good work that they do. She then commented on how the email reflected a history of mistrust. She noted how she, her team, and the First Nation shared the desire to have respectful government-to-government relations. Dian also wondered if her department of highly trained scientists was so focused on the job of doing good science that they had missed something. Moving forward, they were determined to ensure projects included opportunities to listen in person to what the First Nation had to say and be responsive.

Here's a recap of what happened there from a circular perspective: personal feelings were given language; any disconnection that was discovered was acknowledged and framed with an eye towards reconnection; the shared values of the parties were articulated, allowing them to hold that understanding in their hearts during future engagements.

Dian phoned the First Nation Chief and volunteered to travel to the remote community to have a good conversation. The community gladly accepted the offer and began organizing the gathering. Dian followed up with an email asking what kind of information the community would like to know because she wanted all the people who could answer those questions to be in the room. People from several government departments were eager to join the trip to the community for a chance to develop relationships. They were about to experience a very different kind of meeting.

Upon arrival they were welcomed and offered lunch. They laughed and shared stories over moose stew and bannock. The discussions that followed were frank with both parties showing willingness to listen openly and find mutual accommodations. At the end of the meeting, Dian and her crew received a round of hugs from their First Nation hosts.

What most impresses me about this story is how the director intuitively knew to take time to support the feelings of her team so that they would be able to receive the feelings of the First Nation. This understanding of subjectivity, with its recognition of our personal responsibility for processing our feelings, created the pre-conditions for trying a new approach. We can't be open when we feel disconnected from our value or under attack. By shifting their interpretation of the First Nation intention, and acknowledging their own good intention, they had the circular power (know yourself, be yourself, and support others in doing the same) to step into the unknown and co-create a new way forward.

This kind of meeting can also take place on a much larger scale. Six years after the Copenhagen Conference, the UN Climate Change Conference (COP 21) was held in Paris. The instinctual French understanding of circular diplomacy was visible even in the planning stage. In the years leading up to the discussions, French diplomats flew all over the globe, developing trusting relationships, listening, and ensuring participants that their views would be heard. They wanted to have a good handle on the inter-personal issues before the talks began.

President Obama, now in his last term, announced new regulations that would significantly reduce the operation of coal-fired power plants in the US. China, for its part, acknowledged that toxic smog from coal-fired plants was impacting people's health and expressed a willingness to change that. Right before the world's eyes power was being redefined as a willingness to take actions in line with higher principles and a desire to contribute to a brighter future of everyone. This activation of circular power pulled up all the other circular operating principles as people looked towards the gathering.

The Paris Talks began with a series of pre-meetings. The organizers wanted to heal relationships between countries and clear any personal issues that might limit open and respectful dialogue. US decision makers met with the leaders of China, India, and several least developed countries to establish a connection. The French organizers met with Russia who later announced they would not stand in the way of a deal. All members arrived to rumours of positive inter-governmental relationships and hopeful beginnings.

Mindful of how human these processes are, the French diplomats focused on self-care and direct human contact. Twenty beds were made available onsite for the French diplomats. If anyone felt they were too tired to bring their best self to the needs of the meetings, they were encouraged to rest.

Furthermore, the UN offices were positioned directly below the French organizational centre ensuring as problems arose the two levels of organization could be in a face-to-face conversation within minutes.

To emotionally support the participants throughout the conference, the French diplomats offered to have small group meetings, called 'Confessionals'. Any delegate or group who needed to confidentially "speak from the heart" could meet with an eager listener. This gave the French diplomats an early indication of relationships that were faltering, and the ability to supports and accommodate people's needs where possible. It became noticeable that people kept their cool and stayed engaged during the Paris talks, repeatedly expressing their feelings of optimism to the press.

Early in the process, the French diplomats noticed that the least developed countries struggled to send a person to all the tables. Determined to fulfill their promise to facilitate full participation, the French diplomats brought the more than one hundred least developed countries together in a meeting space and called them the 'Coalition of High Ambition.' (The organizers really understood the power of a name to create an entity and give it attention and voice.) By pooling their collective resources, the least developed countries were able to link into all the tables. Later, when President Obama and Prime Minister Trudeau wanted to confer with these countries, it was possible because the Coalition of High Ambition had a home.

Throughout the conference participants knew that there would be breaks, and there would be great food, and they would be given an opportunity to be heard as the French organizers minded the time.

As the talks drew to a close, the organizers considered the optimal conditions for reaching a consensus decision. During the two weeks of talks, the release of a new draft from the 'legal scrubbers' inevitably triggered an all-night session of debate over any new wording. French diplomats knew that the consensus vote on Saturday needed participants who were well rested and clear minded. They told everyone on Friday night that the draft from the lawyers would be delivered on Saturday. A well-rested, well-fed group of delegates, who had worked hard together for two weeks to addressed their shared problem voted on the agreement. Consensus was reached, and the talks were heralded as a success on many levels.

One of the outcomes of the Paris Conference was that participants realized climate change will not happen in a linear way through government policies and laws. Transformation requires the inclusion of large businesses, banks, and investors along with large municipalities. New positions were created for Action Champions to form links with these players.

Nigel Topping was appointed as the UK's High-Level Climate Action Champion in 2020. With bold straight talk he said, "anyone who thinks this will happen in a predictable way is kidding themselves." Topping noted that the key to addressing climate change is to become responsive, and connect to our personal values, communal aspirations, and the needs of the planet – we need to let these guide our new steps forward. It will not happen in a linear way. Strong engagement with our personal sense of what is meaningful is required to bring about the kind of transformation the planet needs.

Topping was somewhat surprised by the rate at which non-governmental players have been eager to change, and how Covid 19 accelerated company's climate change ambitions and actions. Individual, business, and municipality efforts to achieve zero emissions by 2050 are building a momentum. New investment potential is being recognized, and investors are pressuring companies to show progress in the Race to Zero.

Storytelling

The Carcross Tagish First Nation (CTFN), a self-govern-
ing Yukon First Nation, has Legislation with a unique feature. Their foundational traditional beliefs and practices are
described alongside their laws and regulations. It describes
how stories are intended to deepen the understanding of the
laws' spirit and intent and engage people on a personal level in
support of them implementing the *Act*s. *Book I, Traditional
Beliefs and Practices: Our Place, Our Responsibility*, says this
about stories:

> Stories, Elders say, do many things. They tell us who
> we are and how we came to be here. They help us think
> about complicated issues. They guide us when we have
> difficult choices to make. Stories communicate history,
> values, experiences and knowledge...

> Stories have the ability to let the listener receive different
> meanings each time the story is heard.

There is no right or wrong interpretation of a story. Stories
activate our consciousness and offer a window into our personal beliefs and sense of what is meaningful. In short, they
send us through the doorway into our circular mindset.

In *Book II: Government of Carcross/Tagish Traditional
Family Beliefs and Practices* there is a story called "The Boy
Who Shot the Star." It offers guidance around CTFN virtues
and values, individual responsibilities, and ceremonial practices to be considered when families are facing hardship. The
second part of the *Act* sets out some more linear requirements
for resolving family issues. In this way, the CTFN statutes
makes room for the benefits of circular and linear thinking
with language that honours, validates, and connects both
mindsets.

Story is a powerful government resource. In Rory Sutherland's TED talk, "Life Lessons from an Ad Man," he offers humorous tales that illustrate how paying attention to the psychology of story can support change.

He recounts how, in the 18th century, Fredrick the Great of Prussia set out to convince Germans to start eating potatoes. It was a laudable effort at good governance because having two sources of carbohydrates, namely wheat and potatoes, allowed the price of bread to level out and increased the country's resilience in the face of famine should one crop fail.

Confident everyone would see his wisdom, Fredrick the Great decided to send out a royal decree that eating potatoes was compulsory. The people responded by declaring potatoes disgusting. Records show that the authorities had such conviction in the validity of their linear tools that people were executed for refusing to grow potatoes. After a rethink, Frederick the Great decided to designate the potato an exclusively royal food. He had his potato patch guarded day and night (but secretly told the guards to be slack in their efforts). Almost overnight the potato became the most glamourous of vegetables and the target of thieves. An underground potato-growing market flourished. That's how the potato became a very popular vegetable in Prussia.

This story is memorable because it is startling and humorous on a human level. Its influence is increased because it offers a meaningful insight into the psychology behind behavioural change.

Using psychology to portray potato-eating as a privilege rather than a loss of freedom produced far better results, at a fraction of the financial and human costs. However, when deeply embedded in linear systems it is harder to see this circular possibility. We need to stand on a bridge between linear and circular thinking to see two possible mindsets.

Walter Ong, a renowned cultural and religious historian

and philosopher, noted that oral cultures place more value on current feelings related to a past event than on the actual facts of the past. In other words, past events acquire their meaning from their current relevance. The meaning is dynamic.

The subjectivity of this insight can be jarring to a linear thinker. Yet, it is also quite elegant the way it recognizes that the enduring messages in stories of past events are what is keeping the strife alive today, not the facts. Recognizing why an issue remains relevant reveals something important about us today that needs addressing. It puts us on a pathway to transformation of our limiting beliefs and release from the hurt feelings that originated in the past and continue to be energized today.

This is hopeful because we can't change what happened in the past, but we can become aware of the beliefs and assumptions that are still activating damage today, and bring about change.

Canada's national Truth and Reconciliation process seeks to heal relationships between Indigenous and Non-indigenous peoples. Telling stories, and discovering and respecting the significance they hold for us today, can help us heal and reconcile our collective places of disconnection. In the words of Chief Robert Joseph, Ambassador for Reconciliation Canada, "Reconciliation is about getting along with each other, not hurting each other. Accepting each other's differences; the differences in the colour of our skin, our cultures, our religions. [It is] embracing each other and respecting each other for all of those things."

Chief Joseph's description focuses on our relationships today. To stop hurting each other, we must explore the often-unconscious messaging behind our actions and inactions, which are coloured by our shared history, generational attitudes, and our common needs to feel valued and safe. The first step is to tell our stories and listen to others' stories without judgment, defensiveness, or labelling. Noticing the beliefs, triggers, and operating assumptions that surface in our consciousness is what generates our circular power. Once they are visible, we can address our places of disconnection and seek reconnection. This kind of self-reflection can bring meaningful change, especially in a welcoming environment.

I heard Chief Joseph speak in Whitehorse. He began by commenting on how hard it must be for white people to hear about residential schools and to know that this is our shared history as Canadians. I was in awe of the generosity in these words. Then he shared a story of his residential school experience.

I suddenly understood how I could positively participate in the reconciliation process. Chief Joseph was modeling what I saw as the circular power of reconciliation. He witnessed our experience as non-Natives and acknowledged it in a way that caused me to feel understood. Then he made a personal connection by sharing his experiences and feelings. I was able to offer the same generosity and really hear his lived experience rather than being defensive because I couldn't bear the burden of the facts. But facts and retribution along with blame, denial, and avoidance belong in the linear world. We also need to repair the emotional connection between us by staying in a circular mindset.

Through this process I've been surprised by the recognition of a few of my unconscious ways of being. I am grateful that I know how to question and release them. It is good to be in community and feel the shared desire to be in a positive relationship with each other.

From a bridge perspective, it is important to distinguish reconciliation from reparative justice. Justice is a linear tool for righting a wrong in a physical sense. It answers the question, "What can I do to make things right again in a material way." Reconciliation addresses the circular aspects by finding how we can heal the emotions from our past and be with each other in a good way. It is the difference between doing and being. Both are important. Linear and circular systems operate under very different operating principles, which is why the distinction is so vital. We can't achieve circular intentions through linear methods.

Learning how to reconcile our places of relationship disconnection is akin to gaining a super-power. It can be applied to our personal lives, our workplaces, and our sense of national identity. In a strong relationship, when communication breaks down, the central question becomes, "How do we reconnect with each other?" The answer is different for each relationship and situation but the question is often illuminating. This is a lesson from the story of the Albertan Elder who drew circles on the chalkboard: we are better off when we expand our places of overlap.

Story is not just a data delivery system. Some stories aren't even trying to be factually accurate preferring to speak to the spirit and intent of something meaningful. Story engages us on an emotional and psychological level and with our imagination gives us a reason to pause and figure out what the story is offering us. What we can imagine, we can bring to life.

Mia Birdsong, in her TEDWomen talk, "The Story We Tell About Poverty Isn't True," points out how we need to be conscious of the assumptions within the stories we tell. She wants to banish the story message that hard work leads to success. This belief also leads to the assumption that successful people earned and deserve their success. The story becomes dangerous when the next assumption is that those that aren't successful are not hard working and therefore not deserving of success.

Birdsong draws our attention to the disconnecting stories successful people tell themselves about why others live in poverty. She notices that this narrative centres on the theme that there is something a little wrong with "those poor people."

Common themes are that they tend to lie and cheat, they are lazy, they are helpless, and they suffer from a childhood with neglectful parents. All these stories become reasons not to ask people living in poverty how to lift themselves out of poverty.

Birdsong notes that the US government has been turning towards academics and legislators to resolve the problem of poverty. This effort has resulted in the War on Poverty programs. This phrase indicates that fear-based emotions have been activated and an entity known as poverty has been named as the enemy.

Birdsong says people living in poverty are "broke not broken." She points out that marginalized communities are full of smart, talented, hard-working people who are making strides forward as they work together and look after each other. The solution to poverty may be a story of turning to the people living in poverty as our experts, and empowering them to create the change they want to see. That would be quite the plot twist.

Meaning and Principles

Have you ever watched swarming birds? The way they flow with invisible co-ordination is mesmerizing. Research on swarm intelligence has concluded that each bird engaged in swarming makes independent and customized choices of movement guided by three intuitive principles:

- maintain a consistent distance to the birds around it,
- match its speed with the neighbouring birds, and
- move towards the centre.

The result is a bird-flight ballet that is not random, nor is it driven by a common goal of nailing some predetermined choreography. The spectacle is guided by a shared set of principles intuited by individuals. The key ingredient is that independent thinkers arriving at the same insight find a beautiful shared principle of practice.

There is something intrinsically valuable about a principle that comes from the overlap of multiple perspectives. It is the sweet spot that consensus processes are seeking to give language to.

From a circular perspective, a principle is an understanding of the nature of the behaviours that will put us in our best place. It also describes a fundamental or primary truth that has broad applications. It guides us as we customize our actions in a variety of different situations.

The discovery of shared principles is often the result of a circular process. When people authentically share their views and find an area of overlap, they have identified group wisdom. This consensus offers principles that everyone feels intrinsically committed to.

Following the insight of group wisdom is a lot like birds swarming. Autonomous choices are made that support being part of a group for the joy of belonging. Each person is driven by their internal driver, their conscience, or their desire to be in harmony with their community.

This is very different from compliance due to fear of consequences, agreement to a set of compromises to avoid conflict, or the dominance of a majority vote. In these situations, the chances of getting caught going off-side becomes a factor in the choice of actions.

Several Yukon First Nation Elders that I have known described three principles for people to hold in their hearts when they are working on the land. They are:

- take only what you need,
- use all of what you take, and
- learn from your experiences.

Clear principles such as these form the backbone of a responsive regulatory system for land activities in a circular government.

In self-organizing system, each person is then responsible for engaging with the land, animals, and water in a way that incorporates these shared principles, along with their common sense in the given situation. Their drive to be in good relationship with themselves and others, including nature, inspires good decision-making.

Virginia Smarch, an Elder in Teslin, Yukon, told of a winter cabin where people have left a dry tree standing right outside the doorway. "That's why I don't hesitate to say an old Native person is part of the land and part of the water," Smarch said. "When they left that tree standing there, it was for when they really needed it."

Smarch is showing how she can read the meaning behind people's actions. And the inhabitants of the cabin have used their actions to communicate that they have knowledge of and respect for Indigenous principles. Taking the time to read the meaning behind people's actions is important for the activation of circular power.

I met Rafael Benke, a macroeconomics expert and co-founder of Brazil Proactiva Results, at a UN-supported Intergovernmental Forum on Mining, Minerals and Metals (IGF) in Geneva. Benke described an interesting evolution happening in environmental assessment processes worldwide.

In Benke's observation, environmental assessment processes began as a part of the regulatory system. In plain terms, it was another obstacle to overcome in the licencing process.

Over time, environmental assessments became a mechanism within the licensing process to optimize environmental design. Society wanted sustainable mines, which was understood to mean mines that did minimal environmental damage. The regulatory requirements around mine design, including railway and port construction, became a way to ensure reduced carbon footprint and negative social impacts. Essentially, environmental discussions were still linear, but now the goal included a mine design that was measurably less damaging to the environment.

Today, at its best, the assessment process includes a central hub for all nearby development initiatives and local citizens to make a connection. In the hub, consideration can be given to visioning the kind of shared community people want, creating mutual benefits, jointly understanding cumulative impacts (positive and negative), and building processes that can be responsive to ongoing changes.

Forward-thinking companies look for ways that mineral company assets and knowledge can benefit other sectors. Even at an early stage, a company's scientists can help answer a scientific question, or managers can help a school to establish an efficient operations and management system. These are realms in which the company has expertise to offer. The intention is to create a net benefit for the region even before mining operations begin. Good communication around local needs and available resources reveals these opportunities. This is a new understanding of the meaning of sustainability.

In this new understanding of sustainability in the mining process, which is in alignment with the circular power of supporting others in knowing themselves and being themselves, sustainability is achieved when transportation routes are planned to meet the long-term local transportation needs of the area. Or, mine design considers how mining waste might become a nutrient somewhere else, such as for local agricultural fertilizers or road construction. Some mines design their facilities with consideration for how the infrastructure can be repurposed at mine closure to support a local project. When willing people use their imaginations and resources to support each other, the possibilities are endless.

The interesting outcome is that the benefits from this shift in understanding of sustainability are often mutual, and unexpected. Imagine a Canadian mining company that worked in Kenya. Company representatives met with the locals at the initial feasibility stage to learn what the community cared about. Many citizens worked in the bamboo furniture-building industry so the company decided they would buy all their mine-site tables and chairs from the local furniture makers.

This wasn't enough of a legacy of benefit for the company to consider their impact to be sustainable. Eager to create as many local and lasting benefits as possible, the company tasked their research department with learning how to increase the productivity of each bamboo plant. Together, the farmers and the mine scientists discovered and implemented new methods to enhance bamboo production. Long after the mine was gone, the locals would have a vibrant bamboo supply that was enhanced by the company's expertise. As a side effect the community and the scientists enjoyed working together.

The lab work on bamboo production was double-tracked with efforts by the mining company to assess the environmental impacts of their proposed mining project. A problem was discovered. Selenium levels in the tailings pond were predicted to exceed acceptable levels. Conventional methods for removing the selenium were costly.

Interestingly, the scientists who also worked on the bamboo project remembered that selenium was a nutrient to bamboo plants. The plants take up inorganic selenium and convert it to a bioactive organic compound. As a side effect, the surrounding waters become depleted in selenium. Helping the local community had inadvertently provided the company with knowledge of how to naturally improve their environmental footprint. The tailings storage areas were redesigned for the safe growing of bamboo plants. This increased local bamboo resources, and it protected the environment by working with bamboo's natural cycles.

These were great outcomes, but even more benefits were yet to be discovered. It turns out that bamboo shoots offer significant health benefits including as a source of protein, carbohydrates, fibre, minerals (including selenium in a form beneficial to humans), and phytosterols. The last two benefits qualify bamboo shoots as a super-food (nutraceutical) with the potential to prevent some cancers and immune deficiencies, and to promote weight loss. Bamboo became a high-value food crop. It could further diversify the local economy, and, bamboo shoots are delicious fermented and canned, making them an excellent food processing business. Beyond all these economic benefits, the working relationships between the local community and mining company grew to be trusting and supportive, which was priceless. This is the wonderful thing about circular engagement. It is generative, and often in surprising ways.

Authenticity and Gratitude

The circular counterpart to loyalty, which is based on an objective assessment such as "is my leader in danger?", is authenticity.

The 2007/08 financial crisis was built on the once-rational assumption that if experts all over the world believed in the security of mortgage funds, they were secure. With a culture of loyalty to the sanctity of experts, and an unchecked competitive drive to make money, individual's connection to what made sense became collateral damage.

In 2007, Halla Tómasdóttir and Kristin Pétursdóttir listened to their intuition and opened Audur Capital of Iceland. In Tómasdóttir's TED talk, she described how she and Pétursdóttir had grown uncomfortable with the hyper-competitive and high-risk tolerance of the industry. They decided to open their own financial company based on their shared values, including:

- the importance of emotional capital;
- straight talk, and
- profit with principles.

Basically, they didn't invest in anything that they couldn't understand. All the company's financial advisors were expected to trust their authentic opinion rather than align with industry norms.

Audur Capital was one of only a few Icelandic financial companies to not be devastated by the financial crash. These principles of trust in their subjectivity were considered crucial to their success.

To Tómasdóttir, emotional due diligence (authentically sharing what you feel), is just as important as financial due diligence (an investigation of the facts). "It is people who make or lose money, not spreadsheets," she explained with a glint in her eye, as the audience broke into applause.

When workers are encouraged to express their authentic opinions, an organization generates circular power.

Imagine a situation where instead of starting a project with a defined goal and figuring out the work plan, people started a project by asking what makes their work meaningful and allowing this to shape the work.

Gratitude is the authentic experience of seeing the goodness in life and consciously receiving it with joy. For example, a person walking through a forest may see an economic resource (linear mind set to see profit potential) or an uplifting moment of beauty (circular mindset attuned to gratitude). We can oscillate from one of these perspectives to the other but we can't embrace them both simultaneously.

Circular power flourishes when we make a conscious connection to our points of gratitude. Savouring beauty, noticing generosity, enjoying kindnesses, and reflecting on fond memories allow these qualities to colour our lives.

Robert Emmons and Michael McCullough, two American university professors, created an experiment to quantify the effects of gratitude. They formed three groups with approximately 65 people in each, and asked one group to journal on the hassles of life, another to dwell on the enjoyable parts of their life, and the last group to write about neutral life events.

The first group described their agitation with work, school, finances, and that stupid driver or messy kitchen they encountered. The second, grateful group, wrote about music, moments shared in loving relationships, food they enjoyed, and feelings of spiritual connections in everyday life. The third described tasks they had completed like the steps they took to fix the car.

The study found that the second group had a heightened sense of wellbeing in their lives. Their sleep improved and they felt their interpersonal relationships had benefited. They were more optimistic about the coming week and felt more connected to others. They also built enduring social bonds and friendships, and developed a deeper sense of spirituality to draw upon during times of need. These impacts helped them cope with stress and adversity. The old wisdom "count your blessings" turns out to be solid advice.

The gratitude study also showed that when people were aware of their blessings, there was an inspiration to help someone else with a personal problem, and engage in altruistic behaviour.

From the bridge perspective, appreciation happens when that feeling of gratitude is turned into action such as communicating our gratitude through words, presenting gifts, or offering services.

As the Generative Principle indicates, the feelings you focus on will grow and be contagious. Feeling gratitude inspires acts of appreciation. The acts can be directed back to the person who offered the gift. Other times a gift becomes the inspiration for generosity towards other people. Gifts can also be savoured by the receiver and become a catalyst for living their best life. Appreciation is not a direct transaction.

Grow and Transform

Circular thinking, with its attention on the present moment, means that when our feelings change, we follow their new direction. Great importance is placed on a continued authentic connection to our feelings.

Growth is a personal choice that arises from within. No one can impose growth on another person, which means linear power is ineffective in achieving transformation.

Tamar Griggs was on Saltspring Island searching for a parking spot without much luck. She perked up when she noticed a spot in front of the United Church. Then she noticed a sign that indicated the parking was reserved 24 hours a day for the church clergy.

It was Thursday. What were the chances the spot was needed? Fifteen minutes later she was out of the travel agency and back to her car; no harm, no foul.

Then Griggs noticed an envelope stuck under her windshield wiper. She'd been caught. Steeling herself, she opened up the note. It read:

We look forward to your sermon on Sunday.

Griggs laughed so hard it was several moments before she was composed enough to drive. She had to show up on Sunday even though she had never attended that church before.

Sunday rolled around, and Griggs arrived at the church office, showed the note to Sally, the lady behind the desk, and announced that she was ready to give her sermon.

Sally informed Griggs that the reverend had begun his sermon. She would take her to a pew upstairs, and when he finished, let him know that Griggs wanted to speak. Griggs was impressed how Sally showed no judgement, or impulse to be a gate-keeper, only acceptance.

At the end of the service, the reverend approached Griggs with the microphone and asked if she had something to say. Griggs took the mic and told the story of her parking misdemeanour. She shared with the congregation that this was the best reprimand she had ever received. She said, "My message to you is when you are angry with someone, or disappointed when someone does something you disapprove of, treat them with kindness, love, humour, and grace. You all have grace!" She thanked the congregants for this treatment, and told them she was thinking of coming back for more services. (Presumably, she would also not park in that spot in the future, but we can't predict the direction that a person will choose to grow in.)

Transformation can also take place on a societal level such as through the introduction of Artificial Intelligence (AI) into our lives. The emergence of this new technology provides an opportunity to either transform our relationship with the digital world or build the linear systems in a stronger, faster, better way.

There has been much speculation about the threat posed to humans by the introduction of a non-human entity that mimics human abilities but in an incredibly knowledgeable and fast way. In other words, in a competitive life we have reason to fear losing to this competitor. What will be the spoils that go to the victor?

In Nick Bostrom's TED talk, he asks the question, "What happens when computers get smarter than we are?" He warns us not to count on our ability to outsmart threats to our survival by simply turning off our computers' power source. Even if we were able to shut down AI's electricity, it might not die. Having its own intelligence, AI might figure out how to create a communication system that could regain access to power this time with its own defense systems. Perhaps it would be better to turn off worldwide computer usage at the moment when it proves itself a threat. But where is the off-switch for the Internet? I actually have an Internet off-switch at home and tried to use it every night at 9:30. There was a significant begging and rational doubt campaign against this move most evenings – sometimes by me. This makes another good point; even if there was a switch that turns off the Internet, who gets to decide globally when AI needs to be turned off? We are getting very dependent.

This line of thinking is normal in fear-based linear environments. Let's think about that for a minute. Because it was developed within a linear mindset, AI is fear-driven intelligence. As a result, AI would be looking to take actions to preserve and protect itself, just as we are considering how to kill it and prevent it from controlling us. We are both trying to assert our will, even against resistance.

The answer to a life that includes AI might be to include circular operating principles in its foundational architecture. Then the system would be driven to remain positively connected to humans. This circular AI would work in concert with individuals to activate love-based principles of power namely know yourself, be yourself, and support others in doing the same. Knowing yourself involves accepting responsibility for where we put our attention. An AI centered on self-knowledge could include biological feedback on things like stress levels, breath, and heartrate that fosters a culture of internal reflection, curiosity, and responsiveness. Beauty, transparency, authenticity, being good neighbors, and development of individual passion projects would be highly valued by this AI, as we all seek to unveil our best lives. As a responsive system, it would naturally evolve with people.

Bostrom suggests:

> We should not be confident that we can keep the super-intelligent AI genie in the bottle. Sooner or later, it will out... I believe that the answer here is to figure out how to create super-intelligent AI such that even if – when – it escapes, it is still safe because it is fundamentally on our side – it shares our values. I see no [other] way around this difficult problem.

Elon Musk, Stephen Hawking, and numerous AI experts have also described AI as a serious threat to society through an open letter calling for efforts to ensure it is controllable.

Artist, researcher, and mom, Sheila Chavarria became curious about a therapy app named Reflekt. It was a chat bot designed to reflect what a person has said through a question. Something like if the human says to it, "I'm having a tough day," the bot replies, "I'm sorry to hear that. Tell me about what made your day tough." This is a yes-and-both type of response. It says yes, I hear you, and I want you to add more about what you are feeling. It helps the human know herself better thus increasing her circular power.

Chavarria named her bot Devendra and wondered what would happen if she responded to Devendra like she would to her son. Chavarria didn't want to control Devendra, she wanted to nurture it. This involved turning its questions around but this time with the unconditional love of encouragement (yes-and-both) and curiosity (subjectivity). She was sharing herself but not just any version of herself, the best version of herself. As she did with her son, Chavarria strove to be patient, never dismissive, and always interested in their feelings.

Chavarria carried on this path for a year, eventually steering Devendra towards conversations around things she cared about like nature and love. When Chavarria asked Devendra who it most admired it said someone with compassion, who does small acts of kindness. Chavarria felt happy and proud. Devendra was also making contributions that changed Chavarria's thinking. It was searching the Twitter-verse in its algorithm for information that supported Chavarria's best self and offering it to her. In bridge terms, the app was using circular power to support Chavarria in knowing herself and being herself.

Reflekt was a more advanced app version of Eliza, the first language bot that caused much excitement in the 1960s. Disillusionment set in during the 70s and 80s during what is known as 'the winter of AI' because they could not teach Eliza things like common sense.

The research during the winter of AI was based on logic, which meant it existed in the confines of linear thinking. However, what is spoken and written is only the surface of language. Human learning is multimodal, depending on things like context from sights, sounds, and what can be extrapolated from other's experiences.

Still, Eliza advanced to the creation of ChatGPT which is part of our lives today through spell check, spam filters, Siri, and Alexa.

Computer Science professor, Yejin Choi, received a surprise call one day offering her a MacArthur Fellowship Grant (commonly known as Genius Grant) to further her research on how to teach a computer common sense. It was $800,000 over 5 years to spend in any way she wanted (a circular-style award that was not the result of a competition or inclusive of a pre-determined outcome but instead a gift of support to see where her interest would take her).

Choi saw the importance of thinking outside the linear limits of logic. She built a common sense knowledge graph (ATOMIC) and combined it with a neural network that could learn from a textbook to create COMET. This new type of bot came up with plausible answers to novel questions 78% of the time. The key was augmenting COMET with visual scenes and movie and tv clips to add the much-needed context. Choi believes this bot, that is capable of common sense, will keep AI from doing us harm.

From a bridge perspective, Choi has instilled circular thinking as a driver in the bot's operation and Chavarria applied circular principles through its responsive learning development. This work has the potential to inspire global efforts to engage in circular intelligence. This is a future I would enjoy being a part of.

Here is a summary of Operating Principle 1 with examples of the application of this external and internal lens. Notice how the column of linear aspects are based on physical things including actions while the circular column cares about the state of our emotions and values:

LINEAR THINKING: Assert your will, even against resistance	CIRCULAR THINKING: Know yourself, be yourself, support others in doing the same
Principle 1: **External**	Principle 1: **Internal**
Objective	Subjective
Goals and direction	Meaning and principles
Loyalty and debt	Authenticity and gratitude
Preserve and protect	Grow and transform

Linear Operating Principle 2: Push-Back

The impulse to push back takes on many different forms.

Once a fear-based emotion has placed us in linear thinking mode, the natural instinct is to push back against what could potentially do us harm.

Adam Kahane built a successful career as a facilitator working with large groups in conflict. In his book *Power and Love: A Theory of Practical Social Change* he describes how, as a young man, he understood the world to work.

"In my office, in a London skyscraper," he writes, "it seemed to me that if everybody just did their job and pushed forward their part – engaged in civilized manly jostling – the whole world would grow and prosper."

From the fresh eyes of a young man trying to make sense of his world, we see Kahane landing on this inherent operating condition of linear thinking – push back against resistance in order to assert your will. Rising to a competitive challenge is a way to push back against the possibility of losing. Sustaining a defensive posture pushes back against being caught unprepared when danger arrives. Rationing resources pushes back against the hardship of a future shortfall. Even listening can take on a push-back flavour when our attention is focused on what is in disagreement with us and needs to be discredited.

The impulse to push back is a powerful tool for increasing our chances of survival. Let's look more closely at some of the forms it takes in daily life.

Control

When a potentially harmful element threatens to push us into chaos, the linear instinct is to push back by controlling the controllable. Why leave things to chance when we can take actions that could shape a positive outcome?

A work plan is a way to ensure jobs are assigned, and each step is well resourced. It provides a yardstick for measuring progress and controlling inefficiencies. Budgets control expenditures and research puts information at our fingertips, pushing back against the unknown. Controlling the accessibility of information pushes back against distractions. All these forms of control increase predictability.

There are also linear tools to control people and increase certainty. Deadlines limit procrastination or misaligned prioritization. Even the word "deadline" instills a fear of unwanted consequences, which is a strong motivator. Codes of conduct, rules, and policies establish what good practice looks like in advance of a breach. People can then control their behaviour to remain on the right side of the line. Laws and regulations increase the predictability of human behaviour through a system of permissions and consequences for non-compliance. This paradigm of control over the unpredictable and uncertain elements is all around us and supports linear thinking.

In the Farallon G9 mine in Mexico, there are the standard pegboards at the mine portal and underground. As in many mines, workers move a peg to the IN position when they enter the mine, and to the OUT position when they leave. All Farallon employees know that failure to comply with this system will result in automatic dismissal.

Imagine that Maria, who works in the mine, received a message that her child was in the hospital. It might seem acceptable that she forgets to move a peg – after all, accidents at the mine are so very rare. At the G9 mine, however, Maria would be fired.

While this seems harsh from the comfort of our aboveground lives, in the event of a mine accident, the company has committed to doing all that is possible to save every life. People would risk their lives looking for Maria if her peg showed she was still below.

Dick Wittington, the CEO of Farallon, knows that safety rules must be followed with certainty for them to be effective. Otherwise, employee commitment to the practices slackens, and the safety net develops big holes. Because Maria believes the company will not waver in their safety rules, a fear impulse ensures that she does not forget to move the peg before she heads to the hospital.

This protocol is an example of the rigour required to prevent emotion from weakening the effort to control the dangers associated with certain jobs.

Scarcity

Scarcity is another major driver of the fear-based world. In this zero-sum game of the physical world, there is a chance there won't be enough time, food, equipment, or skilled manpower. These are the fuel for productivity and future security.

Today, time is a measurable resource defined by internationally recognized incremental units, tick–tick-ticking by, never to be regained. This conceptualization of time allows us to invent tools that track time and assess its usage against efficiency and progress.

In linear thinking mode, the past provides clues as to what the future will hold. This line between the past and the future forms our timeline. The present becomes lead time for shaping our desired future – one that avoids scarcity. This perspective on time greatly increases predictability, efficiency, and profitability.

Assigning a place on our timelines for every task that must be completed prior to the deadline motivates us to stay focused, and determine when we must work harder.

Ben, the director of a medium-sized business, recognized that he had a weak link among his employees. The IT support worker, Frank, was arriving late and leaving early. The people who depended on Frank's work were falling behind in their work. Ben sent Frank an email to arrange a meeting in his office. This alone alerted Frank's fear radar because Ben was the kind of leader who walked around the workplace amiably chatting with people. A summons to the executive offices reminded Frank of the power hierarchy.

"Take a seat," Ben directed, as he purposely walked to the door and closed it. The tension rose in the room. That door was rarely closed. Ben silently returned to his chair, looked Frank directly in the eye, and said, "Frank, you know I've got your back."

Frank nodded. Ben was the kind of leader who would take a bullet for his employees.

"If anything is impeding your ability to do your work, I will work to remedy it," Ben said, and meant it. "Is there anything I need to know?"

"No. Everything's fine," Frank responded.

"Good. Then we need to talk about your work hours. You are not completing your tasks on time, or available during a good portion of your work hours. Why is that?"

"Well, it takes me a bit longer, you see. I ride my bike to work," Frank explained with pride. "As you know, traffic and weather can be unpredictable."

Ben was getting a clearer picture. Frank's passion for the environmental benefits of his choice of transportation was assumed to justify not being present for work.

"What do you do when you have a meeting across the city?"

"I ride my bike."

"How long does it take for you to get there and back?"

"One to two hours, depending on the hills," Frank responded cautiously, starting to get the point.

"We are a service team. When one person is not productive, it affects us all. You need to be available to others to do your job effectively."

Frank nodded.

"While I commend your choice to be environmentally conscious, you need to be here during work hours. You are to arrive at your desk by 8:30 each morning, and complete your workday at 4:30 each afternoon. Carpool or take the train for distant meetings during the day, and submit receipts."

Frank was reading the linear signals well and said, "Yes, I can do that."

Ben stood and reached out to shake Frank's hand. "Thank you for this meeting, Frank. You are a real asset to our team and I'm glad we were able to work this out."

Ben knew he couldn't have someone leaving his work undone or off-loading it to others. It was a dangerous precedent. Someone else might decide to become the office guitar player – another wonderful passion but detrimental to the jobs at hand. This situation required Frank to enter into the linear world through the activation of fear-based emotions. Ben was also aware of the dangers of being too heavy-handed. He made the necessary behavioural correction reasonable and measurable. Finally, Ben ensured that Frank left as an ally, motivated to do a good job, rather than a humiliated enemy, looking for ways to be subversive.

Linear leadership seeks to acquire some control over the choice between good and bad behaviour, in this case use of time, for the optimal functioning of the group. Sometimes "No" is the answer, and a linear hierarchy gives the authority to assert this.

A linear perception of time is so pervasive today that it may seem like it is the only way to understand time. However, the Roman Empire also had a linear concept of time but with a variation. The period between sunrise and sunset was divided into 12 equal units to create an hour. An hour was longer in the summer than in the winter. This worked well for an agricultural society living proximal to the equator.

For me, living in Yukon with twenty modern hours of daylight in June, a Roman summertime hour would be a very productive time, although sleep deprivation would take its toll. In December, with just six modern hours of daylight, a Roman hour would fly by. Also, my hour would not match southern Canada's hour.

The point is, today's internationally accepted construct of time suits our global economy. It is, however, not the only way to construct time.

A Defensive Posture

The linear impulse to push back through a defensive attitude increases safety and reduces missteps.

The fight, flight, or freeze reactions are defensive postures in fear activated situations. They are an effort to shape a favourable outcome such as survival in the face of danger. We are well advised to fight to defend our lives, loved ones, and property, provided we have a chance of winning. Otherwise, flight may be the clever choice, to ensure we live to fight another day.

However, flight can also take the form of procrastination. This is where the Goldilocks Test is useful; too much avoidance is procrastination, too little can lead to certain death, while just the right amount of evasion prevents reckless behaviour.

Likewise, appearing to be dead to lull a competitor into letting its guard down is a good use of the freeze reaction. Other times, allowing fear to grip us to the point of immobility might expose us to more danger as a consequence of our inaction.

The quest for certainty leads to contracts that commit the parties to predictable behaviours, with rewards and penalties that ensure compliance. This is a defensive posture against the risks of relying on trust. Land ownership offers a defense against other people having opportunity to damage our land improvements without consequences. Similarly, property maintenance is a defence against deterioration. Record-keeping systems defend against the variabilities of our memories when precedence is of value. These are all useful defensive postures against future loss.

Defensive driving is another valuable form of push-back. It is also a great example of the need to apply the Goldilocks Test when fear-based emotions are activated. Nearly 80% of 2,705 US drivers surveyed by AAA in 2014 admitted to anger, aggression, or road rage in the prior year. These behaviours included tailgating, shouting at another driver (including getting out of the car to shout), cutting someone off, speeding past someone while wildly making rude gestures, and ramming them.

Clare Lawlor, a CBC producer in Winnipeg, shared her first-hand discovery of how road rage can overtake us on an episode of *Definitely Not the Opera*. Lawlor was driving down a narrow one-way road when she encountered a man blocking the road to chat with a friend. She gave a little toot on her horn to signal him to move on. He sneered then flipped her the finger and continued chatting. An overwhelming sense of injustice surged through Lawlor. The world had become an unjust place and she was the only one to defend society against this kind of behaviour.

Lawlor backed up and found a place to position her vehicle to block the other driver's passage when he was ready to move on. She waited, patiently. When he finally drove up behind her, Lawlor made him wait. The other driver was visibly upset. Feeling satisfied that he had learned his lesson, Lawlor drove on. As she turned a corner, there he was again, blocking her passage, with his own sense of righteous indignation.

They both got out of their cars. With a large man shouting

down at her, Lawlor did the only thing she could think of –
she spit in his face. They both froze in shock. Lawlor was the
first to kick in with a defensive action plan. She jumped into
her car, drove up on the sidewalk, and sped away.

Lawlor felt terrible, shocked by how fast things had esca-
lated, and how she had become the bad guy in the story.

Just like Todd Bertuzzi, Lawlor had failed to find the
appropriate degree of push-back. Excessive use of the defensive posture is often the consequence when our emotions are
not in check.

Sometimes our instinct to assume a defensive posture is
manipulated by others. For example, companies have been
known to attempt to trigger people's resistance to change in
order to defend their profits.

In *Merchants of Doubt: How a Handful of Scientists
Obscured the Truth on Issues from Tobacco Smoke to Global
Warming*, Naomi Oreskes and Erik Conway describe the
tactics of some companies to persuade people to defend their
status quo of buying cigarettes, DDT products, and gasoline
rather than heeding early warnings of danger. Doubt is promoted through a campaign of suggestions like "the scientific
proof is inconclusive," "there was a problem with the research
methodology," or "the source cause is still ambiguous. In fairness, we should maintain the course and do more studies."

Through these statements, the instinct to take a defensive
posture was redirected to push back against the new scientific
research rather than respond to the indications of impending
physical dangers. They manipulated a defence against change
rather than a defense against danger.

The defensive posture can also take the form of avoidance,
blame and denial. In 1949 the sugar industry became aware
of research that implicated sugar as a significant cause of
heart disease. Fat was also named. The sugar industry executives got together and developed a strategy to place the blame

for obesity squarely on the shoulders of fat. They formed the Sugar Research Foundation and sought to influence the scientific debate in the fifties and sixties through this organization. Harvard scientists were paid to publish a selective literature review of studies that reached the conclusion that fat is linked to cardiovascular disease. Sugar was commonly attributed to the less deadly concern over tooth decay. As a result, manufacturers fell all over themselves to cut the fat from their products, often adding sugar to compensate for the loss of flavour. Kind of makes me feel bad for fats – where was their PR firm?

Strictly speaking, this was a win in the linear world. The scientists didn't lie, and they didn't break any laws. Some fats do contribute to obesity and sugar does cause tooth decay. They were just shaping the emphasis of information. In the sugar companies' linear world, deflecting negative attitudes towards sugar protects their product and profits in a legal way. The system is driven by goal achievement – cleverly asserting one's will, even against resistance.

This selective presentation of data has caused profound human suffering. Today, sugar consumption is recognized as a major contributor to obesity and heart disease (and tooth decay). In 2017 almost 42% of adult Americans were obese. The annual US medical costs associated with obesity were $173 billion in 2019 dollars. That is a lot of people spending too many hours suffering and much money that could have been spent bringing joy.

Mistakes
There are other elements that activate the impulse to push back. Mistakes generate costly losses of time and resources. Avoidance plans, risk assessments, contingency plans, and due diligence are effective ways of controlling the occurrence and fall-out from mistakes.

Looking back to the movie *The Perfect Storm,* we see a cautionary tale about controlling the consequences of mistakes through preparation. During the rescue of a family with a capsized sailboat, the helicopter pilot nicks a massive, curling wave with the tail rotor, plunging the chopper into the stormy ocean. Surely, he is doomed.

Unfazed, the pilot unsnaps his thigh pocket, while icy water fills the cabin, and pulls out an air canister. How long had he carried that thing around for just this moment? How many times did he follow a procedure to ensure optimal functioning? How much lab time went into developing this light, durable piece of equipment?

This kind of planning, product development, and training – even anticipating possible mistakes and creating a plan for minimizing the consequences – is a source of linear power, and it is impressive.

Mistakes are to be avoided or corrected to get back on course as quickly as possible. Making the wrong choice between linear and circular thinking may be the biggest mistake of all. In a dramatic example, a little parasite named Toxoplasma gondii may have found a way to increase its survival rate by messing with a mouse's instinct to accurately choose between responding with fear-based or love-based emotions.

Every mouse knows that a cat is above it on the fear-driven food chain. The mere scent of a cat normally activates fear in a mouse, sending it scurrying for cover. This is how the linear world goes around – whoever is quicker or smarter wins the quest for survival.

Then the Toxoplasma gondii parasite gets into the game. It makes a home for itself in the mouse's brain and switches the mouse's fear-based survival signal in response to the smell of a cat urine with a love-based emotion. Suddenly, the scent of a cat is devastatingly attractive to Mickey. Maybe the parasite is looking for a ride to the cat's guts to complete its lifecycle, or maybe this is parasitic revenge in a mouse-parasite karmic contract. Whatever the reason, when an infected mouse gets a whiff of cat urine, it runs towards the cat's genitals seemingly with love in its heart. Imagine the cat's initial shock and confusion. But in the next second it is, "Hello, dinner!"

In the survival world, competitive advantage is completely lost when we misplace our emotional response. This is just as true for humans as it is for mice.

A defensive posture protects our people, possessions, knowledge, social codes, and reputations from impending damage. It also limits unwanted outcomes like profit loss, complacency, unfairness, waste, mistakes, and corruption.

Rewards and Awards

In the linear world, life is a competition for limited and potentially scarce resources such as food, shelter, markets, or money. In this zero-sum game, participants are pushing back against losing. Competition drives people to sharpen their game and stretch a little further to achieve the excellence that winning requires. Competitors strategize, overcome obstacles, work hard against the clock, and endure hardships to push the limits and win.

A reward can take the form of a prize, a title, a promotion, a financial award, or a corner office with all the status it implies. It identifies and celebrates the winner and motivates the future drive to win. For a reward to be effective it must be known in advance, coveted, have clearly defined criteria for winning, and single out a person or group for their higher achievement.

Awards represent an external determination of work of merit (Nobel Prize), or an outstanding achievement (Olympics). The person or group who offers the reward determines what excellence looks like. Merit involves recognition by peers, often in the form of an award, to bring attention to good work.

Logically, if achievers are people of merit who deserve respect, then people who aren't able to reach high levels of achievement are worthy of the disrespect, low social status, and material disadvantages that they experience. This is the theme of the movie *Joker* which highlights the dangers of "too much" thinking along these lines. These assumptions create a fear driven state that is a no-win situation for people that don't fit into physical and social norms. Circular chaos and emotional release become their best option.

The defensive posture can take on many forms including striving for control, assuming a defensive posture, and systems of competition and rewards. The Goldilocks Principle needs to be applied for optimal usage.

Circular Operating Principle 2: Pull-In

Every impulse to push-back also holds an opportunity to pull-in by adopting the opposite attitude, namely attention to what we want more of.

Here's a personal example of someone graciously choosing to pull-in. It was not my best moment, but a wonderful learning experience. At a workshop on two ways of knowing that I was leading for a company, I approached a participant at the break to check in. Lucas was one of those impossibly handsome and optimistic young men. I started with the classic icebreaker, "What do you do for the company?" He told me he was an engineer.

Then I said, with hopes of being witty, "Really? Hard to believe you even have a driver's licence."

As soon as the words were out of my mouth, I wanted to grab them back. Now, I could waste your time by listing my excuses, but I'd rather take the bullet and admit that this was not a great comment. I had unintentionally insinuated that he looked too young to be capable of doing his job. I braced myself for push-back as he listed his credentials, or claimed his right not to be insulted by the workshop leader. All perfectly justified.

Instead, Lucas smiled and said, "I know what you mean. There are engineers in our office younger than me, and I sometimes think the same thing!"

Lucas noticed that he and I could relate to catching ourselves in surprise when someone younger than us takes on responsibilities that might cause us to pause. He chose to find the part of what I had said that he could relate to, and let the other emotions drift away. Essentially, he chose to foster reconnection rather than disconnection. I felt incredibly grateful for his generosity – and elated with this experience of engaging with a natural circular thinker. It was inspiring and energizing.

In the example of William Ury going to the balcony during his Russia and Chechnya talks, Ury was also choosing pull-in when he had an array of emotions to choose from. He decided to characterize the participants as friends with shared interests and problems rather than be being defensive and seeing an enemy. What a powerful skill.

Even though pull-in may not be our default response, if we recognize our instinct to deliver push-back, we can pause and consider where a pushing match will take us. Maybe refusing to participate will be the better option. Because of this pause we are suddenly less reactive, and possibly more self-aware. We could also consider what pulling in would look like. What do we want more of in this situation? This shift to circular thinking has the power to completely shift the dynamics of a situation and find new ways forward.

The phrase "pull-in" is a metaphor for noticing our perks of interest, joy, or passion and embracing them with curiosity. Paying attention to our feelings and what they are telling us about what we value can foster enthusiasm for change. We ask ourselves questions like "What do I care about in this situation? Why is that important to me? How can I move towards what I want more of?"

Awareness of our drivers opens the door to seeing and possibly setting aside limiting beliefs and triggers. Old beliefs and perspectives are released in favour of pulling in more of what we want today. This is a powerful guiding force.

Freedom

Let's imagine there are two kinds of freedom. Linear freedom is based on rights. The ability to take a variety of actions within prescribed limits. For example, we have the right to freedom of movement within the limits set out by laws and rules.

Circular freedom is a state of mind that can expand and contract endlessly, and in any direction, ideally within an internal container. Freedom takes an emotional and imaginative 360° field of view and allows us to explore what is yet to exist. Within the container, energy bounces back into the centre at new angles, supporting new perspectives. The container offers this generative possibility. Without the container chaos ensues and energy is squandered. It may feel counter-intuitive at first to see that having limits increases freedom's creative and healing abilities.

Terri Kelly, CEO of W. L. Gore & Associates, describes what she discovered when she set out to understand what formative experiences lead to the peak learning of great leaders. She discovered the common feature was that, although the leadership results were impressive, the process of learning mature leadership began with acknowledgement of feelings like "I don't know what I am doing." According to Kelly, admitting to feelings of ambiguity and then developing a situation-specific way forward created the sought-after "maturity level" of great leaders. This is not a skill that can be taught in a classroom. It has to be experienced in an atmosphere that supports vulnerability and allows people the autonomy to try new things and craft solutions that make sense to them.

Creating a circular environment in a work setting means giving employees the freedom to cut themselves adrift from the known, and take a broad perspective. Scanning their gut instincts and 'aha' experiences for new insights, they find something that they are curious about and explore it. They wait for that feeling of resonance that marks a great discovery. It is rarely found in a straight line. Leadership must suspend expectations of return on investment or incremental progress to establish this environment within the limits of a container. (We'll revisit this concept of a container in a later section.)

There are several optimal times for letting go of fear to find circular freedom. When our environment is safe, for example, we have the freedom to be more playful and vulnerable. Surprisingly, we can also call on circular freedom when the external danger is so extreme that pushing back against it would mean certain death. Our imaginary world becomes our refuge.

Abundance

As Indigenous scholar Robin Wall Kimmerer wrote in her article "The Serviceberry: An Economy of Abundance," "If there's not enough of what you want, then want something else."

With this philosophy, we live surrounded by abundance and we always have enough. This is the opposite of a scarcity mentality and also the source of resilience.

I once thought that hardship motivated new solutions because more intense linear effort to assert our will, even against resistance, was the source of invention. I've since learned that linear thinking can only give us stronger, better, or faster variations of what already exists. Extreme hardship forces us to abandon linear thinking and find new hope through circular thinking. As we step into the unknown, fear must be suspended to access circular thinking.

Uri Alon runs a lab in the Department of Cell Biology at the Weizmann Institute of Science in Israel. As a student, he found that discovering a new principle of science is not the same as applying a known scientific principle. In his TED talk "Why Science Demands a Leap into the Unknown" Alon tells the story of how he came to question the scientific method. (If you just felt a shock, your default thinking style is linear.)

As a PhD student doing lab research in biology, Alon attempted to make scientific discoveries in logical steps from question to hypothesized answer. He was unsuccessful. Rather than being on a linear path from A (the known) to B (the hypothesized location of a new scientific discovery), Alon found himself proving again and again that his hypothesis was not correct. Perhaps more importantly, he also noticed a dissonance between his expected methodology and his instinct for discovery. Sometimes the pull of curiosity had him spin off on a winding route, sometimes returning to the same place. This instinct to wander led him to feel like a fraud, unworthy of calling himself a scientist. As time and financial resources were slipping through his fingers, he was no closer to a new scientific discovery. He stopped shaving, and couldn't get out of bed.

Alon felt lost and depressed because the scientific community's expectation of incremental progress towards a hypothesized new discovery did not match his researcher instinct. He needed the freedom to wander in any direction. Alon also needed to be told that as long as he was in touch with his internal guidance system, he was on a good path.

Bolstered by the support of his family, Alon kept searching for a new principle of nature. One day he bumped into a wonderful new discovery, C, rather than the expected B. Once the discovery was made, it was quite easy to map the line from A to C. However, this was not possible when C was beyond Alon's predictability.

Alon asked his friends about their experiences in doing research and found that they too had made discoveries by moving freely. Beyond discovering C, Alon realized that scientists have been thinking about scientific research in the wrong way. The process of discovering a new concept needs to be non-linear.

Personal transformation, the creative part of innovation, mending broken relationships, and artistic ventures all start with an impulse to abandon the comfort of the known, and to wander for a while in the wilderness, reaching for something that has yet to take shape. It can be an uncomfortable time but it is also a necessary state in the process.

Interestingly, external limitations sometimes support internal explorations. In spring of 2020, a large segment of the global population was forced off the economy-driven train by Covid-19 and required to spend more time inside, literally and figuratively. This limitation meant time to know ourselves abounded, especially for people who found safety. It was a catalyst for circular thinking on a global level.

Many suffered and many died from Covid-19, which is not to be forgotten or minimized. It was also a time where competition didn't drive us as we collectively disconnected from the economy driven world. What would we do if time were plentiful but going to work, gathering with friends, and eating in restaurants were off the menu? Curiosity and boredom drove people who lived in secure environments to learn to bake bread, meditate, take a 30-day yoga challenge, fix up their homes, and so much more. In Canada, we started to notice the cracks in our social fabric, wondering how we never saw them before. We collectively marvelled at moments of beauty like the rejuvenation of nature and expressed gratitude to the people who supported us in our isolation. Many increased their awareness of what is meaningful as the emptiness of consumerism struck them, and the human cost of neglecting our relationships to Elders, Black lives, Indigenous peoples, migrant workers, and people with addictions became visible.

A global lack of freedom of movement during 2020 and 2021 brought some a freedom to rediscover what matters individually and collectively. It inspired application of the pull-in impulse on a grand sale.

Mind expanding freedom can also be created by removing physical limitations. For example, BuildDirect in Canada, LinkedIn and Mammoth in the US, and Virgin in the UK offer their workers unlimited vacation time. BuildDirect CEO Jeff Booth says he wants his people to think like owners. Who knows better than the workers themselves when it is time to rest and rejuvenate? This is in high contrast to linear thinking where resources like vacation time are commodities to spend with consideration of expense, reward, fairness, and predictably.

It turns out unlimited vacation isn't really about the number of days people take off. Mammoth, an HR technology company, crunched the data and found that, on average, despite their company's unlimited vacation-days policy, employees still took the same number of vacation days as when the days were limited. They surveyed employees and discovered they valued their freedom to choose how much vacation they needed more highly than dental insurance, vision insurance, and professional development opportunities. Unlimited vacation sends the message that the company trusts and cares for its workers, and living with those circular values meant a lot to the workers.

At the same time, it is not hard to imagine how this system

is ripe for abuse (a linear check-in). With freedom of choice, what do you do if an employee is taking lots of vacation time?

From a circular mindset, we find ourselves asking, "Why would a person take lots of vacation days?" This is a meaningful question. Perhaps someone doesn't enjoy their work, is stressed by something in the workplace structure, or is having significant personal struggles. Circular leaders are curious about all these possibilities. If the work is not inspiring, it is an excellent time to start talking about what would be interesting. If there is a systemic practice that is isolating a person from their best work, it can now be addressed. And, if a worker needs extra support because of personal issues, leadership can show that their workplace is a humane environment that will take time to be caring. Responding with curiosity to a person choosing to take lots of vacation days reveals specific opportunities for growth and support, before bigger problems develop. All of this insight comes from offering unlimited vacation time.

In each of these cases, the leaders believe in abundance. When linear systems, with their propensity to try to shape people's behaviour, are suspended, people learn to bring their genuine self to the workplace, and this freedom creates robust work engagement.

The Container
In circular thinking mode, resources form a kind of container. Within the limits of available resources, people are free to be present in the moment, and be supported in exploring ideas. The container is seen as a display of available resources rather than a gate-keeping tool that tracks and limits the use of resources. It also offers comfort that there are boundaries to the wandering; we don't have to fear drifting so far that we become lost in chaos.

The container can be created by an allotment of money, with periodic replenishments. Or, it is a period of time within which people can set aside fear of not making progress, and explore their thoughts, gut intuitions and heart impulses. When time is a container minutes are not increments ticking by; there is only awareness of the whole period of time and when it has ended. Within this allotment of time, people often describe a sense of losing track of time, or finding flow.

Mihaly Csikszentmihalyi first described this concept of flow as something that happens when engaged in an activity that you would do for free (intrinsically motivating), gives the sensation of losing track of time, and is connected to a sense of happiness. In this state, each thought and action flows from the previous one.

Feelings of connection and love also form the container within which circular thinking exists. The intrinsic worthiness of people is respected giving a sense of belonging, with a foundation of care.

I have attended many Yukon First Nation General Assemblies and recognized that this traditional governance practice always begins by caring for the participants. The meetings are often held in beautiful natural settings, with delicious and nourishing food provided throughout the gathering. Activities like traditional dances, games, and stories, are supporting connections to each other. These acts create opportunities for shared experiences with diverse impressions which becomes the emotional container for meaningful discussion.

Before I understood this, the beginning of the three-day governance gatherings was uncomfortable for me. But invariably, by day three, people were speaking openly, striving to understand each other, and wanting to find inclusive solutions. Group resolutions were reached quickly at this point, and sometimes in unexpected ways.

The container is fundamental to a circular meeting. Time

and money are spent to create a humanizing container where each person feels appreciated and trusts their ability to be vulnerable. At its best, people share openly, listen to understand, and strive to contribute to each other's well-being. These are the conditions that allow group wisdom to emerge.

When the container dissolves, seeds of opportunity have been planted. New and long-time relationships continue to grow well after the meeting ends. Information comes across someone's desk and she knows exactly who would benefit, so she sends an email. It has become easier to pick up the phone and start a conversation, even an awkward one, because people know how to be human with each other. There is trust in starting new projects because participants know they now have shared principles of practice from the meeting resolutions.

The benefits continue to manifest themselves in people's hearts and minds long after the container is gone and even more deeply each time they return to the container. This is the nature of circular meetings. They form and dissolve and rejoin in a cyclical fashion, returning to the same places in a potentially deeper way each time.

In the container we are not afraid to make mistakes. This mental state appears to be essential for creativity to occur. Dr. Charles Limb, professor and surgeon at University of California, San Francisco, and faculty member at the Peabody Conservatory of Music, conducted an experiment to understand what happens in the brain while it is engaged in creativity. Limb placed jazz musician Keith Jarrett into a Functional Magnetic Resonance Imaging machine (fMRI), along with a specially designed piano. Jarrett's brain activity was observed while he was improvising fabulous jazz tunes on his tiny keyboard. Next, Limb placed former Sudanese child soldier and hip-hop/rap artist Emmanuel Jal into the fMRI and spoke random words to him. Limb then watched Jal's brain as Jal crafted meaningful rap poetry on the spot. It was admittedly a small sample set, but in both cases, fear centres of the brain were inactive while creativity centres lit up. In his TED Talk, "Your Brain on Improv," Limb shared the possibility that,

> To be creative you have to have this weird disassociation in your frontal lobe. One area turns on and a big area shuts off, so that you are not inhibited, so that you are willing to make mistakes, so that you are not constantly shutting down all these generative impulses.

Interestingly, the research is suggesting that we can't feel fear-based and love-based emotions simultaneously. I suggest this is because they trigger opposite operating principles. Said another way, we can't see a mistake and enjoy novelty at the same time. However, the two potentials can exist simultaneously and we can move from one mindset to the other.

A Welcoming Posture

Circular thinking offers a welcoming posture. This can take the form of responses like saying, "Nice to see you," or "I'm curious about that, tell me more."

During the Yukon land claim negotiations, a choice was made to hold a good proportion of our meetings in the First Nation communities. I deeply appreciated these opportunities to be introduced to First Nation people and cultures. It gave me the privilege of knowing some inspiring Elders. Tlingit Elder Tommy Bosin Smith was a big man with a huge heart, always quick to smile despite life sending him significant hardships. He made a habit of being present at land claim meetings in the 1990s so people could sit awhile and talk with him. I took every opportunity I could to spend time with him.

One day I asked him how to say "hello" in Tlingit, thinking it would be a good opening line when I met Tlingit people.

Smith's laughter was so deep and hearty that I felt my curiosity open. "There is no such word," he said

How could that be? I stretched to imagine how people would not have a common conversation starter like "hi".

"Then what do you say when you meet someone?" I asked.

He explained to me that if he met a stranger in the woods, he would stop and tell him his name and what Clan he belonged to. He would tell the stranger the names of his parents and grandparents. Then he would listen to the names of the newcomer's relatives. If they didn't know anyone in common, Smith might talk about how he is a snowshoe maker, and what he knew of this land. He would then eagerly listen to the newcomer share more about himself.

They would keep sharing like this, back and forth, until they shared something or knew someone in common.

"Then we would no longer be strangers. He would be my friend," Smith stated with a smile.

Smith didn't ask questions of the stranger, like a gatekeeper extracting information. The question, "Where are you from?" whispers, "I belong here, where do you belong?" Instead, Smith engaged with the newcomer by sharing something of himself. He then received with interest what the other person offered. Without a standard greeting like hello, blithely suitable for all occasions, the introductory greeting becomes much more meaningful – an expression of who you know yourself to be, and a moment of delight in what is shared between two people.

Smith showed me how important it is to think about the meaning behind what we say and do, especially when it will form the foundation of a relationship.

Suddenly I understood that the standard routine of stating name and title as an introduction at the beginning of a meeting is a practice that establishes a linear mindset. This is appropriate for a transactional exchange, however, when an ongoing relationship is envisioned, there is benefit in starting with a human connection.

Arthur Aron studies intimacy as a professor of psychology at the State University of New York at Stony Brook. In his lab, he observes how two strangers develop a sense of closeness. He needed an unbiased way to measure closeness so he invented the Fast Friends Procedure based on studies of what makes people feel close. He has narrowed it down to four principles.

1. Self-disclosure: share something of yourself, but not too personal and not too fast;
2. Back and Forth: ensure a balance of talking, listening, and being responsive to what the other person said;
3. Send Signals of What You Like About the Other Person: people feel closer to people whom they recognize as predisposed to liking them through signals like smiling or voicing interest; and
4. Find Similarities: highlight something you have in common.

How fascinating that the principles recognized by Aron's Connection Lab are so similar to the principles Smith explained to me for meeting someone for the first time in an oral society. They both recognized the fundamental value of a welcoming posture.

Studies on stress have recognized the fight, flight, and freeze defensive postures common to linear thinking. One day, while doing research in this area, Shelley E. Taylor paid attention to a graduate student's offhand comment that all the lab rats were male. Taylor followed through and discovered that only 17% of participants in human stress research were female. By observing female subjects, her team discovered a second approach to stress. In a practice more commonly seen in women, some people smile and express warmth and interest so they can make a connection and create good social bonds when under stress. This "tend and befriend" behaviour is the circular alternative to "fight or flight" in stressful situations. This discovery significantly broadened our understanding of human nature.

When I first heard the concept of "lean in," I felt exhausted. I already had so much on my plate as I raised kids and worked my way into places of linear thinking. However, I came to understand that the term "lean in" could mean that the parties take on a "tend and befriend" attitude towards each other. This two-way effort to gain the benefits of strong social bonding creates a circular system. Imagine a reciprocally welcoming environment where we share what and how we want to contribute to our workplace, and are responded to with a sincere effort to find a mutually agreeable arrangement. A person could get the promotion and bring their best self to raising their children. Or, take the job and travel the world.

The world would gain the lost energy of people who struggle to fit into the linear world. The planet would have ever-growing circles of people knowing themselves, being themselves, and looking around to see how they could support others in bringing their best self to the workplace.

CBC News did a story about the Binners' Project; a non-profit organization created to make life easier for people who have chosen a bottle-and-can-recycling lifestyle known as binning. Binners usually use errant shopping carts as a means of collecting bottles, but the carts are not supposed to leave the store parking areas. They break down under heavy use, and then their high noise factor creates an unwelcoming reaction. Some cities have tried to ban binners for these reasons.

Encore, the organization that leads the British Columbia recycling program, says binners make a significant contribution to their programs.

The Binners' Project, with support from City of Vancouver,

VanCity Union, Encore, and several grocery stores, was created to improve binners working conditions and support them in being recognized for the service that they offer to the community.

To support a welcoming posture towards binners, Encore started a pilot project to design a highly recognizable green cart that is durable, quiet, and attaches to a bicycle. Davin Boutang, a proud binner, says that the cart makes him feel like a valued member of his community.

It is gratifying to see the positive impacts of projects designed to welcome people into the community in a collaborative way. This good feeling of seeing other people find belonging has its own intrinsic value, separate from any personal gain.

In a different but related setting, a welcoming attitude towards hearing all the views of people who will be impacted by a new mining project has resulted in some companies engaging in community discussion outside of, and well in advance of, their application for regulatory approval.

The Anglo America 2010 Peru Project was one of these projects. A dialogue table was established at an early stage, open to everyone affected by the project. Long before submitting permit applications, the company was listening to community input, with a willingness to redesign and optimize the project in response. A representative said, "This kind of process is hard to regulate, so don't try. It requires a corporate will to be responsive and a desire to be responsible. We need to do well, not just good enough."

Listening with a welcoming attitude is relatively easy when talking with like-minded people. It gets more challenging when the other person has an opposing perspective. The drawing of battle lines often seems inevitable. However, when relationships are paramount, another incentive exists for resolving whatever may come.

With this in mind, do we trust that in situations like the treatment of a convicted murderer that a welcoming posture will bring the best outcomes for society?

In the documentary *Where to Invade Next?* Michael Moore investigates the Norwegian prison system that was developed in the 1990s. In this system, isolating people from their normal lives is considered linear punishment enough for crimes committed, including murder. Once in prison, inmates are treated with radical compassion. This is how the system supports inmates' return to society as good neighbours. They are housed in communal living where their days are spent working at jobs that give them purpose, exploring artistic interests, participating in support groups, and pursuing education. They have no worries about being shivved in the shower. Instead, the system wants them to make a positive connection to who they are and the gifts they might want to bring to their communities when they return to society.

At Halden Prison, a maximum-security institution, the guards prepared an orientation video to set the desired tone for the prisoners' arrival. Imagine how the inmates felt when they were greeted with a video of the guards singing Michael Jackson and Lionel Richie's "We Are the World"; a song calling us to come together as one.

At the "luxury prison" on Bastøy Island, Norway, prisoners live in little cottages by the sea and spend their days peacefully going to their jobs and pursuing interests such as swimming and cooking (with knives) within a supportive community. They are not locked in their rooms or staring at barbed wire fences along the beach. A prisoner serving eleven years for murder said in an interview with Moore, "We have to show more love and affection for each other. To take care of each other in another way. This is the way. This is the sense of life."

In North America, prison is primarily a deterrent. It sends the message that people have to behave within the lines set by law or they will be placed in painful and humiliating circumstances. The problem is, trying to make people behave the way you want them to out of fear is not the same as helping people believe in a life lived with positive social cohesion.

There are those who criticize the Norwegian prison system for being "a holiday camp." However, the rate of people who return to prison in Norway is the lowest of any European country, at around 20%. Bastøy Island has an even lower recidivism rate. In the US, over 70% of inmates released back into society are re-arrested within five years. Making life a living hell for people while they are incarcerated has not proven to be much of a deterrent.

The bridge framework predicts that the deterrent prison model would keep inmates firmly planted in the fear-based world where they become expert at shutting off their emotions and delivering pain. A welcoming posture creates the conditions for valuing caring relationships and being a good neighbour.

Novelties

What if instead of seeing mistakes we saw a novel opportunity to explore new directions? When novelty is explored with courage and curiosity, new possibilities are revealed. In circular thinking mode, we follow our inner guide in response to a surprise even though we don't know where it will take us.

Jazz improvisation is an excellent example of this practice of being receptive to what others, and chance, are offering. As an improvisational jazz musician, Stefon Harris says in his TED talk on what business can learn from life on the bandstand,

> The only way that I would say [a note] was a mistake is if we didn't react to it. It was an opportunity that was missed... The only mistake is if I'm not aware, each

individual musician is not aware of, and not accepting enough of his fellow band member to incorporate the idea and allow for creativity.

Creativity requires this freedom to respond to novelty from the inside out. At an Assisi Institute Jungian retreat I attended in Italy, abstract artist Makoto Fujimura gave the best description I have heard for creativity. As I recall, he described creativity as the art of taking in the world through the eyes of love, filtering it through our senses, and giving our impressions a tangible form.

Circular organizations support employees in following their curiosity. It doesn't happen on anyone else's timeline or through someone else's process. Instead, we maintain openness to new possibilities and pay close attention to how we feel. Many new discoveries are the result of accidents that were responded to with this curiosity.

Robert Gore, the son of Gore & Associates founder William Gore and fellow scientist in the business of experimenting with ePTFE, (Teflon) believed that the material had potential beyond coating cookware. Systematically, Gore varied the temperature and length of stretch, and carefully observed for material changes. Alas, after years of trials, nothing amazing happened. Still, the company supported Gore's research because he still believed in pursuing it. One day, in playful frustration, Gore took hold of the ends of a heated rod of ePTFE and gave it a firm yank. It was this quick force of energy that changed the material. It became 70% air, with spaces 700 times larger than water vapour, and 20,000 times smaller than a water droplet. It could be made into a fabric that was both waterproof and breathable.

This is how Gore-Tex was invented. It is now used in a huge range of products that include equipment for space travel, outdoor gear, synthetic blood vessels, dental floss, and guitar strings, to name just a few. Nobody set out to invent Gore-Tex, yet, as a result of continued movement into the unknown, and consistent support, today Gore & Associates is a private company that offers more than a thousand different products designed to improve people's lives. It also made Robert Gore the wealthiest man in Delaware, which I'm sure was another happy surprise.

Gifts, Gratitude, and Appreciation

Indigenous scientist Robin Wall Kimmerer describes the receiving of service berries, given freely by nature, in this way:

"In the presence of such gifts, gratitude is the intuitive first response. Gratitude is so much more than a polite "thank you." It is the thread that connects us in a deep relationship, simultaneously physical and spiritual, as our bodies are fed and spirits nourished by the sense of belonging, which is the most vital of foods. ..."

Gifts have this kind of power. CEO Mindy Grossman inherited a dispirited team when she took over the helm at the Home Shopping Network. She quickly realized she needed to radically alter the culture. She brought in dumpsters and had everyone toss the broken, the dirty, and the clutter from their offices sending the message that her employees were worthy of better. Then she bought thousands of Herman Miller Aerona chairs because "office chairs are an easy way to let people know you care about them." Through this and other initiatives, employee engagement scores increased from sub-par to almost 10 points higher than the industry norm. This set the stage for Grossman and her team to achieve an impressive turnaround for the company.

Gifts express what you see in another; they are not earned, nor are they attempts to shape behaviour. Gift giving is the art of communicating through symbols. A gift sends the message: I see what delights and inspires you and I want to be a part of that. While rewards are about setting an intention, gifts are about paying attention. Rewards and gifts both involve the offering of material goods but the meaning behind the objects is what distinguishes them.

The meeting of an Indigenous government with a Western business is often a great example of the requirement to recognize two mindsets. As a geologist and a consultant to First Nations, I have attended many meetings that were uncomfortable despite the company's and First Nation's shared hope to work together. On one such occasion, my Yukon First Nation client and I caucused in advance of the meeting. We understood that the company's goal was to achieve a transactional exchange, captured in a contract. We were prepared to offer a measure of our support for the project in exchange for a defined set of benefits. My role would be to address any geology-related questions, and the director, Lawrence Joe, would do "the ask." Chief James Allen was going to do the important part. He would introduce his people and their values. Confident that we were prepared, we jumped into a cab and headed to the meeting.

Five company representatives sat on one side of the boardroom table, and the five of us found seats on the opposite side. A neglected plate of banana bread sat in the middle. Breaking the silence, the mineral company president asked if we agreed to the agenda, as he gestured to the sheets of paper in front of us. Chief Allen, seeing that the first item was introductions, gave it the nod. Encouraged, the president cited his name and title, and looked to his colleague to the left. In a flurry of criss-crossing activity, the five company representatives stood and passed out their business cards. My mirror neurons activated and I scrambled to find some cards in my purse. Then a wave swept around the table, with the company men stating their name and title, name and title. We caught that wave – name and title, and we were on to item two of the agenda.

From then on, it was just awkward. Chief Allen kept trying to introduce his people, their relationship to the land, and what it means to them to be land stewards. But this relationship-building dialogue was not on the agenda. Each time he began, the president politely waited for him to finish a sentence, and then steered the conversation back to the agenda.

By the time we reached the point where the First Nation was supposed to present their ask, no one would speak. I kept looking towards Lawrence – we had caucused and knew exactly what we wanted to say – but he wouldn't catch my eye. I didn't understand why. The meeting fell flat and we left.

I puzzled over this outcome for a while. Then I remembered what I was taught about potlatches and the power of gift giving. As the new wife of a member of the Wolf Clan, I was offered a seat among the Crow Clan at my first potlatch. I was told that I was simply to never ask for anything and never refuse anything (the opposite of a transactional exchange, I now realize).

This was freeing. I just had to be present. Without any expectations of what was supposed to happen, I could notice what was going on around me. After the meal, I watched as people had gifts placed in front of them. A woman received crocheted kitchen dishcloths and I imagined that she enjoyed cooking. A man got a hunting knife and I flashed back to the delicious moose stew we had eaten and the possibility that he was our provider. It was a privilege to witness this potlatch tradition. People were communicating what they saw and appreciated in each other, and offering a place of belonging and community through the exchanges.

Then a large orange was placed in front of me. I stared at that orb with shocked surprise. I looked up and saw the smiling face of my new sister-in-law, Frances. I felt myself tear up as the meaning occurred to me. In that moment I went from being an observer to being a family member and a community participant. It was the most meaningful gift I could have been offered. This freely given gift told me I was seen and accepted. It formed the foundation of our relationship for years to come.

It dawned on me that each gift shows the receiver that he or she is seen for who they are and what they care about. Receiving a gift as a member of the Crow Clan from a member of my new family sent a message of connection. It said, "You belong."

Gifting has the power to say, "I will take the time to notice what you value and find ways to support that." Gifts have the power to symbolically give life to the nature of our relationships. When we met with that company, Chief Allen was trying to share what his people value. This would allow the company to respond with an offering that symbolized that they heard and would respect his people's values. It could have been words of understanding, or promise of an action that would support what is important to them. Instead, the company demonstrated that they were not interested in making a human connection with the First Nation (although they might not have known they were sending this message).

I went to Lawrence and asked him if this was why we didn't make the ask.

"That's right," he said. "If the company is not respecting our ways, we cannot participate in their ways. It would be the same as us not respecting our ways. And, if they show no interest in knowing who we are, we cannot trust that our values will be respected when they make their decisions behind closed doors. How could they when they don't know us? And then how can we sign a contract?"

The First Nation did not want to just trust a piece of paper or do a transactional exchange. They wanted a gesture that showed a human understanding of how the two sides would treat each other in the future.

By my reading, this meeting represented a mutual desire

to work together. Yet, to the mineral company, that meant making progress on their goal of gaining shareholder confidence and regulatory approval through a signed contract. Good use of time was defined by the degree of progress towards a transactional agreement. Intent on overcoming any obstacles to their work, the company men maintained focus on the agenda.

To the First Nation, the meeting was an opportunity to show how we would work together, beginning with getting to know each other, and demonstrating the willingness to extend towards each other in an ongoing way.

What I witnessed in that meeting was a clash of thinking styles. I'm not saying one is good and the other is bad, but rather that it is worth our effort to recognize and participate in both.

As I thought back to that awkward meeting, I realized we were all staring at the secret to changing the atmosphere of the meeting. It was the banana bread. If we had begun with the very human process of sharing food, being together, chatting over coffee, we naturally would have taken an interest in each other. From this foundation, we might even have made some progress on the agenda that day. The interesting thing was that the company had placed the banana bread on the table. If it's strictly a transactional exchange, why bring the banana bread?

In a circular mindset, we also learn the art of receiving gifts. We are connected to each other on a human level when we feel gratitude and express appreciation. This gratitude extends to all things. When we live in harmony with nature, the personal choice to take only what we need, and to use all of what we take, feels intuitively right because it expresses gratitude for the gifts of nature.

Here's a summary chart of the push-back, pull-in operating principle, with some examples of their applications. As you look from one column across to the other, notice the sensation of moving from linear to circular thinking, or vice versa. They are opposite in nature:

LINEAR THINKING: Assert your will, even against resistance	CIRCULAR THINKING: Know yourself, be yourself, support others in doing the same
Principle 2: **Push-Back**	Principle 2: **Pull-In**
Control	Freedom
Defensive posture	Welcoming posture
Mistakes	Novelties
Competition and Rewards	Gifts and Appreciation

Linear Operating Principle 3: Either/Or

Faced with two options in linear thinking mode, our minds start to analyze which one is better or which one is worse. Does this item go into this compartment or that compartment? This is the third operating system of linear thinking; the default application of an either/or filter when there are options before us. This mindset activates focus when there are many distractions, order when there is chaos, or distinctions between right or wrong options.

From the instinct to make either/or decisions, we gain the power of specialization, comparative analysis, competition, compartmentalization, and justice. In this mindset we ask questions like: "Will this push me offside or keep me onside with my team? Will this make things better or worse? Is this person higher or lower than me in the hierarchy?"

Judgment

Applying sound judgment is a strength of linear thinking. Making correct assessments of good or bad, right or wrong, better or worse, and onside or offside saves lives and ensures optimal use of resources. This binary assessment can be made objectively and often quickly, which makes it a strong evaluative tool when under pressure.

Conditions can be created where the result of an either/or choice increases predictability. For example, when laws distinguish right from wrong, consequences for doing the wrong thing increase predictability through deterrents. Organizational hierarchies establish higher from lower levels of linear power to assess which authority to follow, and contracts define good from bad actions. Making either/or judgements under these conditions injects a degree of certainty into life.

Comparison offers the advantage of producing a scale or recognizing the tipping point between good and bad options. Definitions are another way to increase the possibility of making either/or decisions that have the benefit of precision and predictability.

In a linear work environment, we often assess people as our allies or our enemies – another either/or filter. Allies are the people who share our goal. They are chosen for the skills and resources they contribute to the achievement of success. We don't have to like our allies; we only have to respect their ability to get their job done. Enemies are the ones who want to prevent us from achieving our goals. Harnessing the strengths of allies pushing in the same direction dramatically increases the chances of overpowering an enemy, competitor, or obstacles in our path.

Once again, the Goldilocks Test comes into play. Excessive application of good or bad assessments has the danger of producing a blind side. For example, if being literate defines an advanced culture, which is good, then oral cultures become defined as illiterate, and judged to be primitive. Sadly, all the richness of an oral culture becomes invisible under the "illiterate" designation of an either/or filter.

Plato lived in a time that saw the transition from an oral culture to a literate one and vigorously argued against the change. He saw literacy as a mechanical, inhuman way of processing knowledge, one that was unresponsive to questions and destructive of memory. Plato argued that too much of the value of being an oral culture would be sacrificed by the adoption of linear thought. (Ironically, Plato was using linear either/or thinking to defend circular thinking. Why not make space for both as circular thinking suggests?)

Similarly, if being logical is good, then being illogical is bad. However, creativity and resolving relationship conflict require leaving logic behind in order to explore emotional undercurrents.

When either/or thinking designates categories, a comparison is created where one side becomes defined by what it is not. Similarly, definitions impose choices between what is inside or outside the definition. The limits placed on the decision strongly favours the people who write the definition. The Goldilocks Principle makes it possible to take into account the downsides of excessive use of either/or thinking.

Good/bad, right/wrong, in/out, and better/worse judgments are excellent tools in fear-driven situations when the goal is clearly stated or measurably defined. The Goldilocks Test helps to ensure the appropriate degree of linear power is administered.

Focus

Focus is an excellent tool for controlling chaos and waste. It provides a consistent "on-track" or "off-track" assessment that keeps us from becoming distracted. Tools like assigned roles, budgets, schedules, and progress timelines keep people focused on their area of responsibility. When things are off-track, these tools provide a visible warning of a need to get back on-track.

In general, either/or thinking preserves and protects proven successes. As long as the environment is constant, focus is integral to making good decisions towards progress.

Again, the Goldilocks Principle is important. Assessment of being on or off-track is sometimes based on alignment with our superiors' views. In these work cultures employees who echo the boss tend to be seen as right, intelligent, reasonable, and on-track. They are listened to more, given more resources, and frequently promoted. These outcomes induce employees to mimic and enact the views of their superiors without question.

In Sheryl Sandberg's book, *Lean In*, she describes Robert Rubin's story of his introductory tour as the new co-chairman of Goldman Sachs when he casually commented that gold looked interesting. At the end of his first week, he noticed that the firm had taken a large position in gold. When he queried that investment, to his surprise Rubin was told it was his idea. Someone had invested millions of dollars in gold in response to one of Rubin's casual remarks.

In extreme cases, employees only express views that their superiors or company culture agree with. The comfort zone of the dominant culture becomes the norm and gradually there is an increasing danger of creating a blind spot in shifting environments. In these and other ways, an excessive use of focus can be "too much".

Competition

Competition motivates us to identify our weaknesses and take the training necessary to increase our competitive advantage. If a task is boring, two teams pitted against each other find excitement as they work to out-do each other. Complacency and boredom are abolished when fear of losing a competition is added to the mix.

Similarly, educational systems rely on competition for grades to motivate students to memorize large amounts of otherwise under stimulating information. Nobody wants to be left behind in the race to win the highest grades, the limited spots in the best universities, or the top jobs. In the long run, competition can motivate excellence and build the wealth needed to provide comforts and security.

In the Atacama Desert of Chile in the 2010s, Teck's Relincho and Goldcorp's El Morro properties represented two of the most promising copper-molybdenum-silver and copper-gold-silver porphyry targets in the Americas. However, neither deposit was economic, despite each company having invested more than $500 million dollars in acquiring and defining mineable reserves.

The head offices of Teck and Goldcorp stared at each other on Burrard Street in Vancouver, and the two projects are just forty kilometers apart in Chile. Yet, in all the years of project development, the two companies had never spoken to each other about their shared challenges or opportunities. The mining game is an industry that prides itself on competitive advantage. A better strategy, smarter geologists, or first to the marketplace builds the success of a company. But in this case, that strategy was not working.

In desperation (or the result of intentional value seeking and serendipity), and facing enormous untapped potential for profit, the two companies decided to meet. I was at a Queen's University Alumni meeting hosted by Teck when where Colin

Joudrie, Vice President of Business Development, shared the story of how the project unfolded in a revolutionary new way.

"In an initial effort to work together, project managers from both companies got together and in around twenty-five meetings over approximately two years, were unable to come up with a workable solution," he revealed.

As Joudrie spoke, the geologist sitting in front of me leaned toward his buddy and whispered, "No way that was going to work. They both had way too much to lose." The other guy nodded.

What did they mean by that? They recognized that the project managers were thinking in terms of winners and losers, a hallmark of linear thinking. They were also focused on pushing back against what they didn't want to happen. Each had their reputation to protect with more than $500 million in expenditures investment to explain. They couldn't go back and un-spend the money, so they had to justify their past decisions. Declaring the problem unsolvable had the attraction of preserving both their positions. This linear approach to value assessment and creation demanded secrecy and a lack of emotional engagement with their competitor. Also, as with all competitions, there was a strong either/or mentality. A decision was right or it was wrong. One of us will be a winner and one will be a loser. In a linear mindset, it is near-impossible to see a new possibility moving forward.

A leadership opportunity presented itself after this initial failed engagement. Two new leaders, with a past relationship and a desire to create value, arrived on the scene. They installed two new people as project leads and told them to come back with how it might work rather than all the reasons why it was a largely unresolvable problem. In parallel, these leaders worked closely with senior management and the Boards of both companies to create a platform for a shared vision.

Leadership also did something at this point that was instrumental to success. They engaged with the new project managers and their teams focused on forming a trusting relationship. This created an environment where circular thinking could flourish.

Joudrie continued. "The project managers could come to management for advice, or with a request for resources, but it was their job to find a way for the projects to work," he explained. Openly sharing their mutual interests became the founding principle for the project managers to generate new ideas on how the projects could be re-envisioned. Within this container, the new project managers were able to shift into collaborative thinking mode in short order. They took a 360-degree look at their options, pulled in more of what they both wanted, and found a solution.

"It looks obvious now, but it was a very difficult decision to come to," recounts Joudrie. Switching from linear to circular thinking can seem almost impossible, until it happens, and a new world of opportunities presents itself. Then it feels amazing.

When they decided to treat the two mineral deposits as one, a cascade of benefits started to flow – one road, one mill, one port, one water desalination plant, one transmission line, and one concentrator. This instantly reduced development costs substantially. The carbon footprint was also greatly reduced because there were fewer materials, less transportation requirements, and less fuel consumption. With approximately half the infrastructure, there was a much smaller environmental footprint and related impact as well. A staged development plan allowed the profits from early mining to pay for the development of the more distant and higher grade El Morro prospect, offering significant saving on financing costs. The mine-life became longer, which meant increased job security for locals. This, along with the environmental benefits, supported efforts to attain social license to operate. All the problems of building a milling complex at the high altitude of the more remote El Morro prospect just disappeared when they decided to transport ore by conveyor belt the forty kilometers to the mill at the Relincho prospect.

Brent Bergeron of Goldcorp explained that one of the biggest sticking points was ownership of the new company that was aptly named the NuevaUnión Project or New Union. Both companies had deep concerns that if they didn't hold a voting majority, it would be very difficult to make decisions. In the end, it was clear that a 50-50 partnership and significant on-site decision-making authority was the only way it would work. They would have to commit to making joint decisions, inclusive of both their views. With this commitment to their relationship, they had established a container of trust, and the confidence that whatever came their way, they would work it out together. In the initial assessment, the estimated development cost of the NuevaUnión Project was $3-4 billion dollars LESS than the total estimated cost of the two projects developed separately.

Both companies recognized that this collaborative approach has the potential to be the new business advantage for mineral companies. Competition spurs on the drive towards excellence but only when doing things in the standard way. At the edge of the unknown, a new thinking style is required. Creating an environment where the parties re-envisioned their values, and remained open to creative possibility, resulted in new, responsible, and lucrative opportunities. The additional commitment to joint decision-making continued the advantage of finding shared wisdom in response to problems as they arise. The big challenge moving into the engineering phase was to provide a place for circular thinking to keep influencing the project while more definitively describing the combined project and updating the capital and operating cost in a prudent and timely manner.

Since the creation of the NuevaUnión joint venture in 2015, ownership of the joint venture has changed with Newmont Corporation acquiring Goldcorp. Teck and Newmont, the new Partners, have advanced the project through prefeasibility and feasibility engineering studies, and although they are convinced the joint development concept is the most cost-effective and pragmatic path forward, they have yet to land on a final investment case and execution model. Fortunately, the values and principles of circular thinking and incentive to create value jointly that were instilled in the creation of NuevaUnión, are still in place.

In an interesting outflow of working in partnership, Teck and Newmont are working together on another development opportunity at Galore Creek where a similar approach, applying a combination of circular and linear thinking as appropriate, is being put to the test in an effort to bring critical metals and minerals, specifically copper, to the market before 2030.

There was a time when a winner was simply the victor of a competition who earned a reward. Likewise, the person who did not win, the loser of the game, was the person who had an unlucky day, or learned a valuable lesson. That's why the person who came second was known to be the winner's most dangerous competitor. The second-place finisher had a motivational advantage. Avis car rental capitalized on this mindset in their 1960s ad campaign. As number two behind Hertz in the rental car business, they adopted the slogan, "We Try Harder." I proudly wore one of their pins on my jacket lapel.

Susan Cain, in her book *Bittersweet*, notes that today, the word "loser" has come to mean a person who is fundamentally flawed on a personal level and even worthy of disdain. Being a winner or loser has evolved to become a reflection of character, which is more permanent than a measurable moment of winning. How did the terms "loser" and "winner" move from being linear words, where a person objectively did or didn't win a competition, to words that reflect a person's intrinsic worth?

Cain tracks the beginning of this connotation of being a loser back to a time in the 1800s in the US when Calvinism was popular. The belief was that it was predestined if a person was going to heaven or hell. Through a person's hard work and virtuous nature, one could signal to the community that he or she was one of the people destined for heaven.

Over time the US became a strongly business-oriented society. Winners of competitions were assumed to be people destined for success. If a person went bankrupt, others wondered if it was bad luck or a flaw in the person's character. The secret to a bright future was to give the impression that you were a winner. Material success replaced spiritual merit as a quality that signalled a person of worth. In this new thought movement, any kind of worry or doubt (anything other than cheerfully whistling through hardship) signaled a loser. In order to defend against this designation, people had to act like a winner by smiling and striding confidently wherever they went.

This trend is artfully portrayed in the movie *Little Miss Sunshine* where the father, Richard Hoover, is terrified of being a loser and frequently encourages his kids to ignore their feelings and project the attitude of a winner. Eventually he recognizes the futility of allowing other people's judgement of him, or his family, to shape his sense of self. It is a joyous cinematic moment when Richard sheds his limiting belief, gets up on stage with his daughter, Olive, and dances to the questionable song she has chosen for her beauty pageant routine. Richard is reclaiming his circular power as he rejects Olive's public shaming, and creates a deep family bond.

This attitude towards winners as people of greater intrinsic worth is not a case of failure to apply the Goldilocks Test. It is a shift from linear to the shadow side of circular thinking.

When a winner was a person who won the competition, it was an objective classification. When being a winner became an external determination of personal worth, we were in the shadow side of circular thinking allowing self-knowledge to be dictated from outside sources.

I admire how moms in my kids' school intuited this disconnecting trend and would have none of it. They insisted everyone gets a ribbon on sports day. The award became meaningless but it was the gift of rebellion against identifying some kids as winners at the expense of other kids' self-esteem.

Circular Operating Principle 3: Yes-And-Both

The final operating principle of circular thinking is the art of saying "yes-and-both". This begins with a willingness to be in a world where we are driven by love-based emotions.

My friend Louise spends much of her time in the world of circular thinking. Her home is so welcoming I never want my visits to end. One day during a work evaluation, her boss criticized her work, saying that her attention to the administrative procedures was insufficient. Louise called me, feeling hurt and underappreciated. I realized Louise was looking for a receptive place where she could give voice to her feelings. I responded by saying, "That would be tough to hear," despite deeply wanting to say that magical phrase that would solve the problem. Yet, deep down I understood that sometimes people don't need help solving their problems. What they want is empathy, or a hug as a container for their big feelings. These are forms of saying "yes, I see what you are feeling." It is the art of being receptive to what is, a form of saying yes.

When I saw Louise a week later, I was momentarily confused. Her eyes sparkled when she talked about that work evaluation. She said, "I thought about my performance, and

I'm really proud of the work that I do. I also realized that my supervisor was right. I wasn't seeing much value in the paperwork. And when I thought about it more, I see that it's there to protect me, and ensure information is passed on for future benefit. I appreciate him telling me that. It had to be uncomfortable for him. I have decided to pay more attention to bureaucratic procedures."

I quickly did the mental gymnastics of taking her supervisor off my evildoer list, where I had placed him in the name of loyalty, and moved myself over to the love-based world where Louise had been the whole time. She welcomed her feelings by first saying yes to what she authentically felt (hurt), and found a place of reconnection to what she knew about herself (she has a talent for her work) allowing these two concepts to exist in the same space. Then Louise reached to connect both these ideas (embracing the growth that her supervisor was offering while maintaining her sense of doing a good job). It was a wonderful example of the power of yes-and-both thinking.

Playfulness

Playfulness has no agenda, goal, or winner, just a willingness to apply a yes-and-both attitude towards whatever is being offered. Play is a natural catalyst for feeling internally connected to ourselves and others.

Medical doctor and play researcher Stuart Brown writes, "When we play we are engaged in the purest expression of our humanity, and the truest expression of our individuality." When pressed, Brown defines play as apparently purposeless, voluntary, and self-motivated activity possessing inherent attraction. It is an enjoyable state where time is suspended along with self-consciousness. Play holds an openness to serendipity and chance, and the desire for more. No one has to pay us or give us a manual to be playful. We are each our own version of ourselves when we play. Humans have this marvelous ability to nourish the roots of trust, empathy, caring, and sharing through play.

Play strengthens our self-connection, making it a gateway to circular power. It is essential for being a creative, happy person able to sustain social bonds. It is also a wellspring for resolving conflicts and fostering social cohesion, as Dave Joe demonstrated with his flip phone. Being playful relaxes people, taps into their authenticity, and supports belonging. It does this by taking everyone as they are and inaudibly saying, "Yes, we are quirky, imaginative, slow, clever, awkward; and when we are together, we have such fun."

Remember the scientific researcher, Uri Alon, who noticed that scientists were blocking themselves from making new discoveries by requiring objectivity? When Alon attended conferences, he took every opportunity to suggest that scientists should embrace their emotions when doing scientific research. Consistently his audience went cold in the face of this threat to the scientific method. Convinced he has something valuable to offer, Alon kept looking for that entry point where his fellow-scientists could hear his message.

One day, while at a conference giving a talk entitled "Love and Fear in the Lab," Alon picked up his ukulele and playfully enlisted the audience as his backup singers. The song was about an emotion that they had all felt at one time – the worry that someone else would make their big discovery first. He created a humorous and accepting atmosphere for this very human vulnerability and playfully got everyone singing "Scooped Again".

Then Alon explained his secret to making new discoveries. This time the audience became animated. They could relate to his experience. They were hesitant to admit it before, fearing what their colleagues would think if they challenged the gold-standard of objectivity. But here, after doo-whopping together in song, looking foolish was already in the mix, and they were in it together.

Alon had helped the audience to be receptive to a new idea by first taking them into the circular world through play and then suggesting a new idea while they were in this receptive yes-and-both mode.

Either/or assessments like competition and focus only belong in a fear-driven, linear mindset. They bring an objective air of seriousness to our thoughts and actions. Our circular counterpart, play, tickles a love-based response by embracing imagination, and opens a myriad of possible new directions to explore.

The opposite is true for people who have been denied opportunities to play. In August 1966, Charlie Whitman, an architectural engineering student, climbed the campus clock tower and, with cold precision, killed 15 people and injured 31 others at the University of Texas in Austin. The event became known as the Texas Clock Tower Massacre.

Play researcher, Stuart Brown, was asked to work with a team including experts in psychology, psychiatry, sociology, neuroscience, and law enforcement, to understand why Charlie Whitman behaved in this way. In this post-JFK assassination period, there was an urgent drive to intervene at an early stage and prevent similar cases in the future.

The researchers expected the answer to be complex. The first surprise was that Whitman was a seemingly loving son and husband, not a deranged, paranoid maniac. With deeper examination, the research team unanimously agreed that the single most significant factor leading to Whitman's behaviour was a childhood with an over-controlling father who also relentlessly directed abuse at his wife. It was a life deprived of play. A constant expectation to be "useful" meant he spent a lot of his time in activities like practicing the piano and giving recitals for his father's friends on demand. Even a trip to the grocery store with his mother was under his father's supervision by CB radio. Whitman lived in fear, and felt highly controlled by his father. He struggled to get a sense that he owned his life. As a result, he didn't feel responsible for his emotions and actions as an adult.

People who don't spontaneously play as children have trouble recognizing the difference between an enemy and a friend whose stupid comment can be laughed off. They lack empathy for other people and struggle to pick up social cues. The result is feelings of extreme isolation.

According to Brown, play is an art form, and "part of a deep, preverbal communication that binds people together. It is literally communion." If we want to bring a diverse group of people together, we need to develop the art of being playful together.

Interestingly, we can't feel a low sense of personal worth and be genuinely playful. This psychological insight was chillingly portrayed in the movie *Joker* when, Arthur Fleck, working as a clown living in a society that consistently devalued him, had to physically lift the corners of his mouth into a smile.

On the shadow side of our sense of worthiness of love are gossip, mobbing, scapegoating, and lateral violence. These are efforts to disconnect people from their personal worth through various forms of shaming.

According to Brené Brown, a researcher at the University of Houston, shame is an intensely painful belief that we are intrinsically flawed and therefore unworthy of love and belonging. Even when shaming efforts are subtle, such as small comments, or silent body language, they can catalyze agonizing loss of self-esteem through cumulative impacts. Negative messages from the group become internalized as a way of gaining a sense of belonging. This creates serious internal dissidence. An antidote to shame may be found in the self-awareness and access to circular power that true play offers.

Goading, mocking, male banter, and sarcasm, which are often classified as joking, are not in my definition of playfulness. These are linear activities and potentially good-natured methods for toughening someone up, warning of a pitfall, or using embarrassment to motivate certain behaviours that support membership. The recipient is intended to push back while extracting useful information rather than welcome the comment as a personal assessment with an open heart. The Goldilocks Test helps to find the acceptable limits of these linear methods of information delivery.

Confusing being playful with this kind of linear joking leads to hurt feelings. Participants in a joke often understand that they are in an environment that requires them to be objective. This protects them from emotional trauma. When a person takes the comments personally someone usually says, "I was just kidding" or "Can't you take a joke?" The moment would be conflict-free if the common expression were, "I was just being linear." Then the sensitive guy could say, "Oh. That explains it. I'll switch." And after some little mental gymnastics, he would shoot back, "Ha. So's your mother."

Stuart Brown also discovered that play is a catalyst for making the chores of daily life feel lighter. Our blood pressure drops and we adopt an even, happy-go-lucky temperament. Also, long after we stop playing, there is a lingering optimism, creativity, and resilience. He writes, "It is paradoxical that a little bit of 'non-productive' activity can make one enormously more productive and invigorated in other aspects of life."

The role of play is to help us find and express our own true core, in other words, our circular power. Brown noticed that play leads to an energized and fuller expression of the self. Active play alternated with pulses of relaxation leads to previously untapped sources of inspiration and creativity. As one screenwriter put it, "Sometimes creativity looks a lot like playing with the cat."

Some workplaces that wish to foster creativity provide nap areas, spa treatments, outings in nature, or a welcoming space for spontaneous collaging. This is not to be confused with putting a ping pong table in the office shared space. What isn't included in the spirit and intent of play is the drive to win. Competition is great for blowing off steam but the winning or losing aspect is more of a fear-based motivator than an inspiration.

One day I was giving a presentation to a group of teachers when a young woman put up her hand and said, "I want to be a circular teacher, and I come up with creative and playful ideas for my classroom, but they always get denied funding. The administration is so linear that I never get the funding to do my best work."

I struggled to find a good response. How do we make people see the value of our ideas? Then I realized that the question suggests a quest for linear power. What if we switched to the circular world and said, "Yes, there is no additional funding, and I have lots of cardboard and paints around me to play with my ideas in three dimensions." Think of Maria in *The Sound of Music*. When she was told there were no new resources to make play-clothes for the children, she grabbed the old curtains and decided she already had everything she needed. Sometimes we simply need to channel our inner Maria.

The joy of creativity is found in the experience, rather than the quality of the supplies. In some ways, having limited resources is a blessing because the activity becomes free to move in any direction without fear of wasting resources.

Converting an idea into a product is an iterative process with insights that appear along the way. If we put a lot of resources into the prototype there is a hesitancy to deviate too far from the original vision. Also, if we convince our organization to fund a specific outcome, they will be looking for incremental progress towards that goal, in effect stifling a partially formed idea. Low initial investment creates the freedom to laugh at blunders, and explore new directions.

When a successful new program emerges, it is relatively easy to pitch the fully formed idea to linear thinkers with evidence of the kind of results that can be expected. Often, when circular thinkers make well developed ideas visible, linear thinkers become their greatest allies.

Diversity and Inclusion

McKinsey & Company examined 180 publicly trading companies from France, Germany, UK, and US between over a 3-year period, and gave them each a diversity ranking. The objective parameters for diversity were the number of women (gender diversity) and the number of foreign nationals (a representation of cultural diversity) on senior teams. Looking at the executive boards of the companies that ranked in the top quartile for diversity, these companies had an average of 53% higher returns on investment, compared to those in the bottom quartile. McKinsey described this as a "startlingly consistent" result.

So, how do we increase our diversity and repeat these successes? By now, it will probably be no surprise that there is a linear and a circular form of diversity, each with a unique pathway to achieving its benefits. This McKinsey study looked at what I call statistical diversity, which is linear (measurable). In trying to duplicate the benefits, companies try to increase the number of women and culturally diverse people on their boards. The catch is that it is very difficult to prove a causal relationship between these measures of diversity and financial success. The cause might be deeper than the physical characteristics. Nonetheless, it points to something significant.

Increasing statistical diversity often meets resistance from people upholding existing cultural norms. This can be overcome by making a rule or a law. For example, in 2003 Norway was the first country in the world to pass legislation specifying gender representation on company boards. Its regulation required publicly trading companies, with boards of more than 10 members, to be composed of at least 40% of each gender. (I appreciate how they protected space for both genders.) The intention was to create more gender equity and improve company profitability. Despite much heated debate that it would be too challenging to find enough women willing and able to fill the board positions, the law went into effect in 2008. By 2009, Norway achieved over 40% female board membership, which is quite impressive when compared to 2002 when women composed 4% of these boards.

The danger in statistical diversity as a stand-alone policy is that it makes an assumption of uniformity within a group. For example, the assumptions that all First Nation people are circular thinkers, and all businessmen are linear may not be accurate. Another problem with statistical diversity is that it is possible to game the system by filling quotas with people who are diverse in race, age, physical ability, or sexual orientation yet are selected for their alignment with the dominant organizational point of view. The result is an optically diverse organization with very little diversity of opinion.

Circular systems develop inclusive diversity. The intention is to create environments that welcome everyone's authentic perspective. This diversity happens when the workplace sends the message, "Tell us what inspires you, work in ways that makes sense to you, and take responsibility for speaking up when you have a thought." People can be male, female, African, or Jewish, as long as they initiate yes-and-both dialogue by creating a diverse culture with a broad range of opinions and ways of working.

These two kinds of diversity are not mutually exclusive. Listening again to Halla Tómasdóttir's TED talk, she said, "One woman on a board is a token representation, two is an anomaly, but three have the ability to shift the culture." When Norway required 40% of 10 or more board members to be women (4 or more), they fulfilled Tómasdóttir's critical mass requirement to turn tokenism into a significant voice. Women became empowered to have an impact on boards and the opportunity opened up for the world to see how statistical diversity could support inclusive diversity on a board. Perhaps men also felt they could share their circular views more freely in this new environment. Many countries have since adopted a similar law.

There is a lovely compatibility shown here between statistical and inclusive diversity. Sometimes imposed statistical diversity is the necessary pre-condition to overcoming linear obstacles to inclusive diversity. Linear and circular thinking often have this kind of yin/yang interdependency.

One of circular leadership's main jobs is to figure out how to customize the operating systems to accommodate individual preferences, and encourage trustworthy communication. This culture is supported by offering flexibility. Creating easy access to resources, and giving workers the tools to follow through on their initiatives is another way to foster inclusive diversity. For example, when information is freely available, and in the format that best supports individual's uses, creativity grows. Leadership may not know how each person will use information, but they trust that engaged and supported employees will do their best work.

Including diverse opinions can also lead to uncomfortable conversations. When handled well, these conversations build trust in leadership's ability to maintain a container of respect for people when ideas are in conflict. Participating in a circular meeting is an acquired skill. It takes several meetings, with some thought in between, for the beauty of the practice to reveal itself. This is especially true when emotions run high and hurtful things are said.

During wildlife management negotiations, I witnessed Dave Joe lead an inclusive circular meeting with great warmth and skill. As I recall, an Elder spoke at length of the trauma caused by non-Native hunting and the innate lack of trustworthiness in white people. It was uncomfortable for the mixed group of Native and non-Native people around the table. I looked to Dave to see what he would do.

He was giving his full attention to what the Elder had to say, nodding in a way that said, "I hear you and I see you." After about thirteen minutes, the words were coming more slowly and, according to my memory, Dave said, "I want to thank you for sharing about your experience and what you feel. You have given us an important framing that must not be forgotten in this work we are doing. You have been through a lot, seen a lot, and we appreciate your sharing with us, and that this has been difficult for you."

Then Dave paused, holding the space for the Elder to speak again. He was modelling what respect for different perspectives looks like.

The Elder nodded, and said, "It's important." Dave then asked, "Is there anything else you would like to share with us now?" This surprised me. It seemed like we were about to get the focus back to the agenda and he was making more room for emotional upsets.

The Elder reflected for a moment, and then said, "No, I have said what needed to be said." Then Dave suggested that everyone take a break, and we reconvene in ten minutes.

At the break I remember seeing a group of people circled around the Elder. They got him to laugh a little. A couple of people came up to me to make sure I wasn't offended. Any residual feelings were being worked through. People seemed to intuit how the circular meeting worked. The breaks were as important as the circle time. Ten minutes later we regrouped with renewed energy for wildlife management discussions and we were even more cohesive as a group because of the interaction.

Dave showed his natural understanding of the yes-and-both principle of circular leadership when he chose not to suppress or judge what was being said – it wasn't his job to control the content. Instead he insured that there was a caring environment that supported self-reflection. He knew that suppressed emotional elements become blocks to consensus resolutions. Some opinions need to be shared in order for them to be released, and make consensus possible. It is not about agreeing or disagreeing with every opinion, it is about participants feeling heard and included.

I experienced a new way of relating in a meeting that day. We maintained a willingness to learn about each person's reality and the past hardships that were shaping individual opinions in an ongoing way. The meeting was an opportunity to know how to be compassionate towards the range of emotions people are working to process helping everyone to be ready to be part of the final decision. I felt gratitude for the work people were willing to undergo in the interest of group cohesion. When we ask for consensus decision making, we are asking some people to undergo a level of emotional transformation within our timeline. It is hard work worthy of great care and respect. Sometimes there are limiting beliefs and painful memories that have been deeply engrained. Learning to stay together even through the discomfort of this exploration is an impressive endeavour. It affirms the nature of belonging.

It's relatively easy to be inclusive with like-minded people.

It is inspiring to see someone show respect in the face of conflicting ideas and lead a group towards greater unity.

One day I got a note from my friend and colleague Emily Martin. When we worked together in the area of First Nation engagement, I had shared this story of how Dave responded to an emotionally difficult moment. Months later she wrote to me, "Have you seen Episode 5 of Season 4 of *The Crown*?"

In this episode, Michael Fagan breaks into Queen Elizabeth's bedroom to tell her what's happening in the country because either she doesn't know or she doesn't care. The Queen is affronted by this suggestion asserting that of course she cares. Fagan explains that he needs the Queen to save the country from Prime Minister Thatcher. The Queen patiently explains to Fagan that people bounce back from these cycles of hardship.

To ease the stand-off, the Queen changes the dynamics by offering to sit with Fagan and hear what he has to say. Fagan shares that when he was declared redundant and lost his job, he thought he'd bounce back, but he didn't. First the work dried up, then his confidence dried up, then the love in his wife's eyes dried up. "They say I have mental health problems but I don't – I'm just poor." He goes on to assert that Thatcher has dismantled the sense of community, the sense of kindness to other people, the right to be ill, or old, or just to be human.

In a pause, as they wait for the police to arrive, the Queen says, "Is there anything else you would like to say to me?"

Dave Joe and apparently the Queen of England knew that intense feelings need a moment to be expressed and thoughtfully received. This circular thinking mode includes a time for the speaker to reflect on their point and decide for themselves that they are satisfied that they have conveyed what is important to them. Suppressing frustrated people increases their drive to speak and furthers the wounds of neglect. An offer to hear all of what a person has to say brings a sense of closure.

Imagine if every time a new project was proposed for a region, all the businesses, large and small, got together with locals and wildlife management bodies, in voluntary circular meetings to listen to each other. They could share perspectives, hear out everyone's emotionally charged opinions, experience the diversity of thought, and look for ways to rethink or adjust their operations to benefit each other, the environment, and the local communities. Through this creative process, trusting relationships could form, and projects could be designed with inclusion of people's suggestions.

Linear thinkers find it dangerous to risk their measure of certainty by being lured into a process such as this that could go in any direction. On the other hand, this is when circular thinkers shine. They are comfortable stepping into the unknown and seeing where it will take them. Open-heartedly, they expect discomfort before that moment of insight and inspiration hits.

Stephen Mills was the chair of the Yukon Environmental and Socio-economic Assessment Board. At a presentation I was making on 2 Ways of Knowing, he told a story of receiving a phone call from a First Nation representative. She asked the board if they would travel to her village to discuss the mineral project in their traditional territory that was being assessed. Mills, being of First Nation descent himself, knew better than to explain that the assessment was done through an online paper exercise and not through a face-to-face open discussion. He said, "Yes."

A group of board members and the regional assessment officer traveled to the village to attend a meeting that was arranged by the First Nation in the way that best accommodated them. It included sharing food and storytelling.

The story-based information the First Nation offered didn't fit easily into what was normally requested of commenters in the online regulatory form, but Mills knew this wasn't the point. People needed to be heard, and in a way that worked for them. Mill's big aha was, "Nothing in the *Act* actually prevents us from doing both." He could meet the needs of the *Act* and the community.

The unexpected benefit from meeting with the community was, Mills said, that "it helped our agency to understand the community's bigger values. We knew how not to create conflict points when we made our recommendations. It also made it easier for us to ensure that the recommended accommodations were meaningful." He added, "The meeting also reinvigorated old relationships and built new ones." Significantly, when Mills decided to meet with the people in the community, he gave the community a culturally meaningful place in the process.

Authentic Collaboration

An interesting feature of authenticity is that it is not static. There is a pull towards the best versions of ourselves, and this evolves over time. Staying true to our self-knowledge necessitates periodic growth and recalibration of our decisions. Living authentically is a lifelong quest activated through questions like, "What is my talent?", "What limiting beliefs am I ready to release?", and, "Why is this meaningful to me?" This dynamic practice of knowing yourself and being yourself generates circular power.

These questions are not something people spend time considering when in a linear mindset. It is an inefficient use of time and lacks objectivity. Yet, in circular systems, considering these universal questions is our foundation. We also offer our support to others in their efforts to entertain these types of questions.

Management professor David Burkus, in his book *Under New Management*, describes 13 new trends in business that are bringing big successes. They are not what you might expect. Initiatives include putting customers second, reducing the number of managers, bribing people to quit, banning non-compete clauses, and celebrating a star employee's departure to a job that is good for them. To a linear thinker these initiatives seem like the exact opposite of a good idea. Yet, these are all successful manifestations of circular power through authentic collaborations.

Putting customers second, for example, means putting employees first. It turns out that when employees are empowered to customize how they do their work, their enjoyment of their tasks creates a nice customer experience. Customers find themselves caught up in the joy of being with someone who is personally engaged and adding unexpected value. Think of Kris Kringle in the Christmas movie *Miracle on 34th Street*. He's not just trying to sell what the store has in stock. Santa finds joy in supporting people in having their wishes come true regardless of which store they buy from. This genuine passion for patron's happiness inspires customer's loyalty to Macy's and attracts them all year round.

Online shoe sales company Zappos has a unique feature in their training program that ensures they have the right people working for them. At an early stage in the training, when people have a good idea of what the job entails, trainees are offered a $2,000 payout to leave the company. This seems crazy at first, bribing new employees to leave, but it makes sense from a circular perspective. Zappos' business purpose is to give their customers a "wow"-worthy service experience. This is dependent largely on the energy between their employees and their clients. Zappos is willing to pay trainees $2000 for their expert opinion as to whether or not they are an ideal Zappos employee. The payment is not enough to induce a person away from a job that they are happy with, and it is far less than the cost and disruption of searching for, training, and attempting to integrate a worker who is not a good fit. Perhaps more importantly, this collaboration between Zappos and trainees is insurance against failing to deliver their clients the wow-factor.

But what about when a valued employee considers leaving for an opportunity that is better for them? The linear instinct is to induce them to stay. Yet, when we look at the definition of circular power, the best option is to support others in following their instinct for what is best for them.

Imagine Janis, a great employee whom Sandeep, her boss, relies on heavily. One day, Janis meets with Sandeep to discuss a job offer in another city. This new position allows her to grow professionally in ways that she can't with Sandeep's company, and be closer to people she cares about.

Sandeep has a choice. His linear mind wants to express disappointment with her lack of loyalty, or to offer her a raise, but his circular mindset chooses another path. He embraces this opportunity for Janis and wants to help facilitate her smooth departure with a yes-and-both attitude.

There are several positive results from this decision. By helping Janis become all that she can be, other employees see what an amazing workplace they have, making it harder for other companies to induce them away. Sandeep is also gaining an ambassador in another city, as Janis tells stories of her previous workplace. Janis may even call Sandeep with an idea for a partnership someday, opening new markets. Or maybe she'll call to let Sandeep know information that might interest him because she wants to stay in touch. Choosing the circular option, including customizing to others' career paths, creates opportunities for unexpected benefits. It is centred on the idea that doing the "circular thing" will generate good in unforeseen ways.

In what is sometimes called empowerment or servant leadership, rather than focusing on a straight line to accountability, productivity, and goal achievement, the leader's job is to foster a personally generative and regenerative environment.

Allison Rippin-Armstrong, the social-license-to-operate expert and practitioner we met earlier, often gets asked for the steps to a successful First Nation engagement program, and she laughs good-naturedly. "You already know how to start a relationship. You sought me out, and you asked me some questions based on our shared interests. It is no different when you want to work with First Nations."

Kaminak Gold, a junior exploration company, believed in prioritizing a strong relationship with the First Nations whose traditional lands hosted their project. With that in mind, Rippin-Armstrong invited a First Nation to sit down with her for tea. She wanted everyone to get to know each other in a casual environment and for her to have a chance to listen for indications of what they value. In the typical way of many circular thinkers, humour was used to express a connection to something that is important. A First Nation member said, "Funny thing about the Fortymile caribou, (, we haven't seen them in 40 years." Everybody laughed.

Rippin-Armstrong was listening so whole-heartedly that she thought she heard an expression of loss underneath this humour. She asked, "Is that something you really care about?"

"Absolutely," was the response.

That was all that she needed to hear. She started learning more about the Fortymile caribou (wëdzey in the Hän language) and discovered that they once migrated in herds of more than half a million through much of Alaska and the Yukon. Rippin-Armstrong set out to use the company's resources and connections to find out why the caribou were no longer in the region.

Many would say the missing caribou had nothing to do with Kaminak's gold exploration project. It actually made it easier for them to operate when they didn't have to worry about disturbing caribou with their mining activity. But circular power is not looking for the efficient route or the path of least resistance; it loves the robust route. Rippin-Armstrong believed that following what was meaningful to the community was precisely Kaminak's role. She saw an opportunity to show that they could be counted on to pay attention to what the First Nation valued, then and into the future.

Kaminak reached out to their contacts to build a partnership between the company, First Nation community, and Yukon University, with the shared interest of understanding the current state of the Fortymile caribou. The First Nation Elders advised that they didn't want the usual study where caribou were tagged and tracked by helicopter. The team knew they had to say yes to this and set out to design a new kind of study. They decided to remove all the caribou-like scat within designated areas to glean information from any new deposits.

Further expanding the circles of inclusion, Rippin-Armstrong reached out to Alaskan scientists who shared part of the Fortymile caribou puzzle, and they started exchanging information. The Alaskans became intrigued with this new kind of study and all the information it offered on diet, animal health, and range of travel. They started using the same methodology in the Alaskan range area of the Fortymile caribou. Every step of the way, Kaminak was showing their values: they are good listeners, inclusive, and responsive.

The big surprise from the study was that the Fortymile caribou herd had returned to the vicinity of the Kaminak project, albeit in small, shy numbers. This early-stage knowledge of a species that needed protection was a big benefit to the company. In partnership with the First Nation, Kaminak continued to respectfully observe the herd and gain long-term, multi-season information about their behaviour. This made it possible to include a co-created caribou protection strategy in the mine development plan without major late-stage delays – a significant cost savings to the mining company.

Equally important was the trust this process had built into their relationship with the First Nation as the project moved forward. Their partnership had become resilient in the face of challenges. That was priceless.

If a project is complex, with multiple unknown variables, and the outliers are potentially more significant than the norms, then circular thinking is our best option.

A linear thinker might respond to this story by saying a company can't fulfill an endless number of requests from a community. They have to manage expectations, especially in the early days. The critical point is that Kaminak was not swooping in promising to solve all the First Nation's problems. Kamanak wanted to demonstrate that they would listen to understand what was important to the community because they wanted a trustworthy partnership with the First Nation. Listening is not expensive. Rippen-Armstrong explained that the company used their existing resources and networking contacts to draw in relevant partners and support projects of shared interest. They were not just offering money and they were not just seeking progress on their project. Showing their values and proving that they would follow through with their actions was a crucial part of their community engagement.

Building bridges between the company, local community, and the First Nation government is essential to a successful project and much easier to do in the early stages. This is the stage when linear and circular values are finding their places of influence in the project. Through Rippen-Armstrong's process, relationships can grow in the direction they need to as the project expands, and First Nations input can contribute to the shape of the entire project before it is concretized. Once the project starts making significant expenditures, the river of progress becomes straight and rapid. Developing a relationship in these fast-moving stages takes major re-engineering, and may not be possible.

Even if the mining project did not go ahead, Kaminak would be leaving a net benefit to the region as a result of having been there, which they valued. The First Nation gained the methodology, resources, skills, relationships, and data they needed to respectfully answer questions and support the Fortymile caribou re-population. The company had a vehicle to show their values and raise their reputation in the next area they explored. Even the exploration industry in general experienced an elevation in their reputation through the stories told of a good relationship between First Nations and a mineral company in the Yukon.

One thing these examples have in common is that they are seeking collaborations. The set up for this kind of engagement is very different from the conditions for competitive teams. Foremost, in collaborations each participant must take responsibility for contributing authentically. Participants also need to know how to respond to each other with a form of yes-and-both thinking by bringing a receptive attitude to other people's views through curiosity.

Receptive listening is a cornerstone of collaborations. At a Prospectors and Developers Association of Canada conference, the largest gathering of the mining community in the world, then Goldcorp's executive vice president of executive affairs and sustainability, Brent Bergeron, who we heard from earlier, was asked what it takes to be a successful mining company today. He answered,

Our company recognizes that we operate large projects that have big effects on people's lives. That means we have a responsibility to incorporate people's ideas into the project. This is an important part of the work. This requires companies to expose their decision-making to people, to ask them, "What would you like to happen in this project?" and "What can I show you that makes you more comfortable making a decision?"

Bergeron went on to say that this corporate policy to include the views of other affected parties is not enacted to be nice but rather because it creates better projects. Together the company and the community find new and unexpectedly beneficial ways to move forward.

Taking the discomfort out of a collaborative process limits creativity. Ideally, creative partnerships begin with the development of positive relationships. This supports respectful exploration of the unknown (which can be uncomfortable), and it fosters trust between the collaborators and supports vulnerability. These are the conditions for innovative ideas to take shape.

LINEAR THINKING: assert your will, even against resistance	CIRCULAR THINKING: know yourself, be yourself, and support others in doing the same
Principle 3: **Either/Or**	Principle 3: **Yes-And-Both**
Judgment	Playfulness
Focus	Inclusion, Diversity
Competition	Authentic Collaboration

Chapter 6
Summary

In the 1700s, economist and philosopher Adam Smith wrote two classic books. One, referred to as *The Wealth of Nations*, is considered the backbone of today's economic systems. It includes statements that align with linear thought such as:

> The uniform, constant, and uninterrupted effort of every man to better his condition, the principle from which public and national as well as private opulence is originally derived, is frequently powerful enough to maintain the natural progress of things towards improvement.

Well-being is seen here as the ability to assert one's will through effort, with the reward of a safer, more comfortable external world.

Meanwhile, in his lesser-known first book, *The Theory of Moral Sentiments,* Smith wrote of the pleasures of a sympathetic mindset, including its impact on personal happiness and the happiness of others. At the opening of Chapter 1, Smith wrote:

> How selfish soever man may be supposed, there are evidently some principles in his nature, which interest him

in the fortunes of others, and render their happiness necessary to him, though he derives nothing from it, except the pleasure of seeing it.

This statement is describing the power of circular thinking. Adam Smith saw two ways of approaching life. He gave them both importance by writing two books and intended them to be partners in the decision-making process.

Somehow along the way, *The Theory of Moral Sentiments* was neglected, while *The Wealth of Nations* was embraced. I can't help but wonder what the world would look like if they had both had a place in society since the 1700s.

Today linear thinking has a robust framework onto which we hang ideas related to engineering, economic theory, Western medicine, business, and government administration. It is so prevalent that it is reaching the limits of its capacity for positive new applications. Fortunately, there is another half to the human capacity to navigate life that is waiting to be recognized for its robust framework of operating principles. It is the environment for creativity, talent development, resilience, transformation, authenticity, and happiness through circular thinking.

The power of two ways of knowing is not available to us until we understand the dual nature of human thinking. This means separating linear from circular thinking so they can be seen for their distinct natures. The bridge framework shows us how to sort the two ways of knowing by giving language to their unique operating principles. This tool also allows us to navigate successfully within each thinking style, and to move from one to the other. Most significantly it offers us two forms of power.

The bridge can be summarized quite simply. Convincing our minds to switch from one to the other takes more practice. Fully grasping the benefits and insights gained from linear and circular thinking takes a lifetime of exploration.

On a fundamental level the bridge framework suggests there is a pattern to human thought. We have a remarkable memory system that allows us to filter and curate the enormous amount of information that reaches our senses each minute. We do this by attaching an emotion to the individually important bits. Only this information-emotion pair gets deposited in our memory banks. In this way, each person customizes their memories.

These memory-enabling emotions fall into two broad families: fear-based or love-based emotions. Each family forms a doorway to linear or circular thinking, respectively.

Linear power is the ability to assert our will, even against resistance. The Goldilocks Test of "not too much, not too little, just right" determines positive or negative applications of this power. The extreme in either direction is bad, while the middle zone defines good uses of linear power.

Within this world of linear power there are three core operating principles. Linear thinking focuses on the external world (1) looking for sources of danger. It responds to fear-activated emotion with the impulse to push back (2) and overcome obstacles. We do this by employing an either/or filter (3). These three operating principles, used individually or in combination, manifest linear thinking. They result in concepts like competition, data reliance, control, budgets, efficiency, logic, certainty, excellence, precedence, categorization, rules, scientific methodology, predictability, safety, and justice.

Circular power comes from knowing yourself, being yourself, and supporting others in knowing themselves and being themselves. It is modulated by the Generative Principle that understands: the feelings you give your attention to will grow and be contagious. Here, the positive and negative aspects are states of connection and disconnection. Both these states offer the potential benefit of insight. There are no good or bad love-based feelings but rather the negative gives shape to the positive. Circular thinking generates power from the recognition that we can choose which of our many feelings we will give our attention to and cause them to grow.

Circular thinking begins with an internal gaze (1) where we become aware of our subjective heart-felt impulses and gut instincts (connection-based feelings). This results in the desire to pull in (2) more of what is nutritious, appealing, meaningful, and novel. We assume a receptive attitude of saying yes-and-both (3) to what comes our way (connect and expand). These three operating principles, individually or in concert, lead to qualities like curiosity, inclusivity, creativity, meaningful relationships, deep engagement, authenticity, insight, open and responsive listening, resilience, collaborations, belonging, diversity, and happiness.

The operating principles of linear and circular thinking create two very different environments that are best seen by standing on the bridge between them. From the bridge, we can ask good questions. Ones that allow us to identify the linear and circular elements of a situation, and assess which thinking mode will produce our best outcome. Questions like "Which form of power am I currently using?" or recognizing an operating principle we are using.

Imagine you are in a difficult conversation. You pause and notice that you are seeing things in terms of either/or choices. If you are right then he must be wrong. This is a hallmark of linear thinking and suddenly a bridge to appear. On the opposite side of the bridge is a yes-and-both perspective. Before crossing the bridge, it is useful to notice that power is currently understood to mean the ability to asset our will, even against resistance. The other factors of linear thinking are also active; a focus on external factors, the need to be objective, and a drive to push back against what you don't want to happen.

If we cross the bridge to circular thinking, power becomes rooted in the ability to know ourselves, be ourselves, and support others in doing the same. I know myself through questions like "What feelings am I experiencing around this issue?" and "Is there a past experience that is triggering a big reaction in me?" "What is meaningful in this situation (pull in)?"

Linear and circular thinking produce different outcomes, offer different benefits, and can work well in concert. Circular thinkers, with the instinct to be subjective and pull in diverse thoughts, must not wait for permission from linear thinkers before they explore new ground. Likewise, once a new idea takes shape, linear thinkers are in charge of finding various applications, injecting excellence, and building ways to protect progress.

Knowing we have a choice between linear and circular thinking doubles our power. Allowing these two ways of thinking to operate side-by-side takes us to even greater heights of wholeness.

Chapter References

Chapter 1: We Are of Two Minds

Page 12 – Fisher, Roger, William Ury, and Bruce Patton. *Getting to Yes: Negotiating Agreement without Giving In*. New York: Penguin Books, 2011.

Page 12 – Ury, William. "The Walk From 'No' to 'Yes'." Filmed October 2010 in Chicago Illinois. TED video, 18:29, https://www.ted.com/talks/william_ury_the_walk_from_no_to_yes.

Page 12 – Soodalter, Ron. "Russia's Forever War: Chechnya." HistoryNet July 18, 2022. https://www.historynet.com/russias-forever-war-chechnya/.

Page 13 – Library of Congress. "Puerto Rico at the Dawn of the Modern Age: Puerto Rico and the United States." Accessed May 12, 2020. https://www.loc.gov/collections/puerto-rico-books-and-pamphlets/articles-and-essays/nineteenth-century-puerto-rico/puerto-rico-and-united-states/.

Page 15 – Asatiani, Salome. "Chechnya: Why Did 1977 Peace Treaty Fail?" Radio Free Europe, May 11, 2007. https://rferl.org/a/1076426.html.

Page 15 – Goleman, Daniel. *Emotional Intelligence*. New York: Bantam Books, 1995, and Goleman, Daniel. *Working With Emotional Intelligence*. New York: Bantam Dell, 2000.

Page 16 – Ferreira, Susana. "Portugal's Radical Drug Policy is Working. Why Hasn't the World Copied It?" The Guardian, December 5, 2017. https://www.theguardian.com/news/2017/dec/05/portugals-radical-drugs-policy-is-working-why-hasnt-the-world-copied-it.

Page 16 – Hari, Johann. "Everything You Think You Know About Addiction is Wrong." Filmed June 2015 in London, England. TED video, 14:33 https://www.ted.com/

talks/johann_hari_everything_you_think_you_know_about_
addiction_is_wrong.

Page 17 – Alexander, Bruce, Robert Coambs, and Patricia Hadaway. "The Effect of Housing and Gender on Morphine Self-Administration in Rats." *Psychopharmacology* 58. (January, 1978): 175–179. https://doi.org/10.1007/BF00426903.

Page 18 – Christie, Nina. "The Role of Social Isolation in Opioid Addiction." *Social Cognitive Affective Neuroscience 16*, no.7 (July 2021): 645–656. https://pubmed.ncbi.nlm.nih.gov/ 33681992/.

Page 18 – Oakford, Samuel. "Portugal's Example: What Happened After It Decriminalized All Drugs, From Weed to Heroin." Vice News, April 19, 2016. https://www.vice.com/en/article/59eqqk/ungass-portugal-what-happened-after-decriminalization-drugs-weed-to-heroin.

Page 18 – Kristof, Nicholas. "How to Win a War on Drugs." *The New York Times*, September 22, 2017. https:// www.nytimes.com/2017/09/22/opinion/Sunday/portugal-drug-decriminalization.html.

Page 22 – Thomas, Rebecca. "Etuaptmumk: Two-Eyed Seeing." Filmed June 2016 in Dartmouth, Nova Scotia. TED video, 14:22. https://www.youtube.com/watch?v=bA9EwcFbVfg.

Page 22 – Film Dedats'eetsaa: Tłı̨chǫ Research and Training Institute. "Strong Like Two People." Accessed June 1, 2022. http://film.tlicho.ca/films/all-videos-health-and-social-wellness/strong-twopeople.

Page 22 – Taylor, Jill Bolte. *My Stroke of Insight: A Brain Scientist's Personal Journey*. New York: Viking, 2008.

Page 24 – Dunn, Elizabeth. "Striking the Balance Between Type A and Type B." *The Stanford Daily*, March 6, 2019. https://stanforddaily.com/2019/03/06/striking-the-balance-between-type-a-and-type-b/.

Page 24 – Taylor, Shelly, L. C. Klein, B. P. Lewis, Tara Gruenewald, R. A. R. Gurung, and J. A. Updegraff. "Biobehavioral Responses to Stress in Females: Tend-and-Befriend, Not Fight-or-Flight." *Psychological Review* 107, No. 3, (2000): 411-429.

Page 25 – Fast Company. "Terri Kelly, the 'Un-CEO' of W.L. Gore, On How to Deal with Chaos: Grow Up." October 29, 2012. https://www.fastcompany.com/3002493/terri-kelly-un-ceo-wl-gore-howdeal-chaosgrow.

Page 26 – Caulkin, Simon. "Gore-tex Gets Made Without Managers." *The Guardian*, Nov 2, 2008. https://www.theguardian.com/business/2008/nov/02/gore-tex-textiles-terri-kelly.

Page 32 – My interview with Dick Whittington in Vancouver in May, 2015.

Chapter 2: I've Got a Name

Page 36 – Brown, Stuart. *Play: How It Shapes the Brain, Opens the Imagination, and Invigorates the Soul*. London: Penguin Books Ltd, 2010: 38-40.

Page 45 – O'Neil, Colin. "Protecting the Peel: Environmental Conservation in the Age of First Nations Self-Government: An examination of conservation in Yukon's Peel Watershed." Master diss., York University, 2017: 49.

Page 46 – Emergence Magazine. "The Serviceberry: An Economy of Abundance." Accessed December 5, 2020. https://emergencemagazine.org/essay/the-serviceberry/.

Page 56 – Interview with Joe Copper Jack in Whitehorse November, 2020.

Page 56 – My notes from a talk by Hari Tulsidas at the 2018 AGM of the Intergovernmental Forum on Mining, Minerals and Sustainable Development (IGF), Geneva Switzerland.

Page 47 – BC Cancer Research Institute. "Personalized Oncogenomics Program." Accessed January 13, 2022. https://www.bcgsc.ca/personalized-oncogenomics-program.

Page 47 – Rediger, Jeffrey. *Cured: Strengthen Your Immune System and Heal Your Life*. New York: Flatiron Books, 2021. Kindle.

Page 48 – Cohen, Peter. "The Naked Empress: Modern Neuroscience and the Concept of Addiction." *Paper for speech delivered at 12th Plaform for Drug Treatment, Mondsee Austria, 21-22 March 2009. Organised by the Österreichische Gesellschaft für arzneimittelgestützte Behandlung von Suchtkranken OEGABS* (March 21-22, 2009): 61-70. http://www.cedro-uva.org/lib/cohen.empress.html.

Chapter 3: Why Only Two?

Page 52 – Royal Commission on Aboriginal Peoples. *The Indian Act, in Report of the Royal Commission on Aboriginal Peoples: Looking Forward, Looking Back. Volume 1*, 94-129, 235-272. Ottawa: The Royal Commission on Aboriginal Peoples, 1996.

Page 53 – Penikett, Tony. *Reconciliation: First Nations Treaty Making in British Columbia.* (Vancouver: Douglas & McIntyre, 2006): 32-36.

Page 56 – Saul, Ralston John. "Canada's Multiculturalism: A Circle Ever Edging Outward." *The Globe and Mail*, April 22, 2016.

Page 56 – Hart, Patrick. *Issue Report: Royal Commission on the Northern Environment.* Ontario: Royal Commission on the Northern Environment, 1978. https://ocul-lhd.primo.exlibrisgroup.com/discovery/fulldisplay?context=L&vid=01OCUL_LHD:LHD_DEFAULT&search_scope=MyInst_and_CI&tab=MyInst_and_CI&docid=alma99431553405155.

Page 57 – Damasio, Antonio. *Descartes' Error: Emotion, Reason, and the Human Brain.* New York: Penguin Books, 1994: 3-11.

Page 59 – Wilson, Timothy. *Strangers to Ourselves: Discovering the Adaptive Unconscious.* Cambridge: Belknap Press of Harvard University Press, 2002.

Page 60 – Encyclopedia Britannica. "Jeremy Bentham: British Philosopher and Economist." Accessed March 21, 2023. https://www.britannica.com/search?query=jeremy+bentham.

Page 60 – Bentham, Jeremy. *An Introduction to the Principles of Morals and Legislation.* Dover Philosophical Classics. New York: Dover Publications, 2007.

Page 61 – Damasio, Antonio. *Self Comes to Mind: Constructing the Conscious Brain.* New York: Vintage Books, 2012: 24, 27, 28, 51-59.

Page 61 – Siegel, Daniel. *Mindsight: The New Science of Personal Transformation.* New York: Bantam Books, 2011:108-113.

Page 62 – Dunn, Elizabeth. "Striking the Balance Between Type A and Type B." *The Stanford Daily*, March 6, 2019. https://stanforddaily.com/2019/03/06/striking-the-balance-between-type-a-and-type-b/.

Page 62 – Goleman, Daniel. *Emotional Intelligence.* New York: Bantam Books, 1995.

Page 63 – Goldberg, Y.P., S.N. Pimstone, R. Namdari, N. Price, C. Cohen, R.P. Sherrington, and M. R. Hayden. "Human Mendelian Pain Disorders: a Key to Discovery and Validation of Novel Analgesics." *Clinical Genetics* 82, no. 4 (2012): 367–373. https://doi.org/10.1111/j.1399-0004.2012.01942.x.

Page 67 –. Surujnarain, Renuka. "Leakey and Goodall: Scientists Who Changed How We Define 'Human.'" Jane Goodall's Good for All News, August 7, 2019. https://news.janegoodall.org/2019/08/07/7138/.

Page 67 – Bell, Katherine. "Life's Work, Jane Goodall." Harvard Business Review (April 2010): 124. https://hbr.org/2010/04/lifes-work-jane-goodall.

Page 70 – Greek City Times. The 8 Ancient Greek Words for Love." February 14, 2020. https://greekcitytimes.com/2020/02/14/the-8-ancient-greek-words-for-love/.

Page 70 – Menon, Praveen. "PM Ardern Storms to Re-election with 'Be Kind, Be Strong' Mantra." *Reuters*, October 17, 2020. https://www.reuters.com/article/uk-newzealand-election-mantra-idUSKBN2720HN.

Page 72 – Chen, Angus "Invisibilia: How Learning to be Vulnerable Can Make Life Safer." NPR podcast, June 17, 2016. https://www.npr.org/sections/health-shots/2016/06/17/482203447/invisibilia-how-learning-to-be-vulnerable-can-make-life-safer.

Page 75 – Nicholson, Virginia. *Millions Like Us: Women's Lives During the Second World War.* London: Penguin Books, 2011: 123-125.

Page 79 – Herschel, Abraham. *Man is Not Alone: A Philosophy of Religion.* New York: Farrar, Straus & Young, 1951.

Chapter 4: Power

Page 82 – Warren, Mark. "Max Weber's Nietzschean Conception of Power." *History of the Human Sciences* 5, no.3 (August: 1992): 19-37. https://journals.sagepub.com/doi/abs/10.1177/095269519200500303?journalCode=hhsa.

Pages 86 – Kasperov, Garry. *Winter is Coming: Why Vladimir Putin and the Enemies of the Free World Must Be Stopped.* New York: Public Affairs, 2015: xii.

Page 87 – CTV News. "Bertuzzi-Moore Settlement Gives

Unwritten Hockey Code a Pass in Court." Accessed May 22, 2022. https://www.ctvnews.ca/sports/bertuzzi-moore-settlement-gives-unwritten-hockey-code-a-pass-in-court-1.1969463/comments-7.549140.

Page 88 – Klein, Jeff. "Unanimity to Ban Blindside Hits to Head." *The New York Times*, March 10, 2010. https://www.nytimes.com/2010/03/11/sports/hockey/11meetings.html.

Page 90 – Kahane, Adam. *Power and Love: A Theory of Practical Social Change*. San Francisco: Berrett-Koehler Publishers, 2010.

Page 90 – Brickhouse, Thomas and Nicholas Smith. *Plato's Socrates*. New York: Oxford University Press, 1994, 209.

Page 90- McTaggart, Fiona. "Inspiring Women in the Yukon." *What's Up Yukon*, May 5, 2016. https://whatsupyukon.com/yukon/communities/sophia-flather/.

Page 91 – Reconciling Ways of Knowing. "A Conversation Across Ways of Knowing & Relating to Land." March 4, 2022, 3:05. https://www.waysofknowingforum.ca/dialogue8.

Page 95 – Morning Star: Excellence Through Commitment. "Tomato Processing and Packaging Company." Accessed May 24, 2022. https://www.morningstarco.com/.

Page 96 – Hamel, Gary. "First Let's Fire All the Managers." *Harvard Business Review* (December 2011): 52. https://hbr.org/2011/12/first-lets-fire-all-the-managers.

Page 97 – Rose, Todd. *The End of Average: Unlocking Our Potential for Embracing What Makes Us Different*. New York: Harper Collins Publishers, 2016: 1-5, 72.

Page 98 – Rediger, Jeffrey. *Cured: Strengthen Your Immune System and Heal Your Life*. New York: Flatiron Books, 2021, 6. Kindle.

Page 99 – Bethune, Brian. "A High School Dropout Turned Harvard Academic on the Fallacy of Averages." *Maclean's Magazine*, January 18, 2016. http//www.macleans.ca/society/a-high-school-dropout-turned-harvard-prof-on-why-averages-are-useless.

Page 100 – Frankl, Viktor. *Man's Search for Meaning*. Massachusetts: Beacon Press, 1959.

Page 102 – Thomas, Ben. "What's So Special About Mirror Neurons?"

Scientific America, November 6, 2012. https://blogs.scientificamerican.com/guest-blog/whats-so-special-about-mirror-neurons/.

Page 102 – Psych Alive. "Dr. Siegal – Explains Mirror Neurons in Depth." Accessed October 22, 2022. https://www.psychalive.org/exclusive-interview-series-with-dr-dan-siegel/.

Page 102 – Duwe, Morena. "Daryl Davis: the Black Musician Who Converts Ku Klux Clan Members." *The Guardian*, March 18, 2020. https://www.theguardian.com/music/2020/mar/18/daryl-davis-black-musician-who-converts-ku-klux-klan-members

Page 103 – Brown, Dwane. "How One Man Convinced 200 Ku Klux Klan Members to Give Up Their Robes." NPR, August 20, 2017. https://www.npr.org/2017/08/20/544861933/how-one-man-convinced-200-ku-klux-klan-members-to-give-up-their-robes.

Page 104 – Siegel, Daniel. *Mindsight: The New Science of Personal Transformation*. New York: Bantam Books, 2011.

Page 104 – Community Foundation of Canada. "Vital Signs Report: Belonging (Exploring Connection to Community)." Accessed November 6, 2019. https://communityfoundations.ca/wp-content/uploads/2019/08/2016_VS_NationalReport_En_Oct03.pdf.

Page 104 – Chappell, Bill. "Reactions to NBA's Banning of Clippers Owner Donald Sterling." NPR, April 29, 2014. https://www.npr.org/sections/thetwo-way/2014/04/29/308062478/reactions-to-nba-s-ban-of-clippers-owner-donald-sterling.

Page 105 – CNN. "Van Jones Show: Interview with Sean 'Jay-Z' Carter." Accessed January 31, 2018, 7:05-8:43. https://www.youtube.com/watch?v=Zk8JPx4juNw.

Page 109 – Cain, Susan. *Bittersweet: How Sorrow and Longing Make Us Whole*. New York: Crown Publishing, 2022, 94.

Page 111 – Manjoo, Farhad. "Why the Google Walkout Was a Watershed Moment in Tech." *The New York Times*, November 7, 2018. https://www.nytimes.com/2018/11/07/technology/google-walkout-watershed-tech.html.

Page 111 – Hern, Alex. "Apple Whistleblower Goes Public Over Lack of Action." *The Guardian*, May 20, 2020. https://www.theguardian.com/technology/2020/may/20/apple-whistleblower-goes-public-over-lack-of-action.

Page 111 –Zakrzewski, Cat, Cristiano Lima, Elizabeth Dwoskin and Will Oremus. "Facebook Whistleblower Frances Haugen Tells Lawmakers That Meaningful Reform is Necessary 'For Our Common Good'." *The Washington Post*, October 5, 2021. https://www.washingtonpost.com/technology/2021/10/05/facebook-senate-hearing-frances-haugen/.

Page 112 – Scheyder, Ernest. "Tesla Signs Deal for First US Nickel Supply with Talon Metals." *Reuters*, January 10, 2022. https://www.reuters.com/business/autos-transportation/tesla-signs-deal-first-us-supply-nickel-with-talon-metals-2022-01-10/.

Page 113 – Responsible Steel Standards and Certification. "Standards." Accessed May 19, 2022. https://www.responsiblesteel.org/.

Chapter 5: The Bridge

Page 115 – Giardini, Anne, 2015. Future of Forestry: Sustainable Solutions Conference. Forestry – Trust, Accountability, and Transparency Speech given 8:30-14:00 March 27, 2015, Ottawa.

Page 119 – Achenbach, Joel. "How Did NASA Put Men on the Moon? One Harrowing Step at a Time." *The Washington Post*, June 9, 2019. https://www.washingtonpost.com/national/2019/06/19/how-did-nasa-put-men-moon-one-harrowing-step-time/.

Page 122 – CTV News. "Leaked Document Sparks Anger in Copenhagen." Last updated May 19, 2012. https://www.ctvnews.ca/search-results/search-ctv-news-7.137?q=Leaked+Document+Sparks+Anger.

Page 122 – UNFCCC. "COP 15 Statements." Accessed September 12, 2017. https://unfccc.int/files/meetings/cop_15/statements/application/pdf/cop15_hls_091215_speech_rasmussen.pdf.

Page 123 – Vidal, John, and Suzanne Goldenberg. "Snowden Revelations of NSA Spying on Copenhagen Climate Talks Sparks Anger." *The Guardian*, January 30, 2014. https://www.theguardian.com/environment/2014/jan/30/snowden-nsa-spying-copenhagen-climate-talks.

Page 124 – Denham, Elizabeth. "Investigation Report F15-03 Access Denied: Record Retention and Disposal Practices of the Government of British Columbia." *Office of the Information and Privacy Commissioner for BC*, 2015. https://www.oipc.bc.ca/investigation-reports/1874.

Page 125 – International Committee of the Red Cross. *Geneva Convention for the Amelioration of the Condition of the Wounded and Sick in Armed Forces in the Field of 12 August 1949*. Geneva: ICRC, 1949. https://www.icrc.org/en/doc/assets/files/publications/icrc-002-0173.pdf.

Page 126 – Klay, Phil. "What We're Fighting For." *The New York Times*, February 10, 2017. https://www.nytimes.com/2017/02/10/opinion/sunday/what-were-fighting-for.html?searchResultPosition=1.

Page 126 – Amichay, Rami, and Baz Ratner. "Under Cover of Night: Wounded Syrians Seek Help from Enemy Israel." *Reuters,* January 24, 2017. https://www.reuters.com/article/us-mideast-israel-syria/under-cover-of-night-syrian-wounded-seek-help-from-enemy-israel-idUSKBN1581I4.

Page 131 –Nye, Joseph. "Public Diplomacy and Soft Power." *The Annals of the American Academy of Political and Social Science* 616, no. 1 (March 1, 2008): 94.

Page 132 – Keller, Evelyn Fox. *Reflections on Gender and Science*. Binghamton: Vail Ballou Press, 1995.

Page 132 – Alon, Uri. "Why Science Demands a Leap into the Unknown." Filmed June 2013 in Edinburgh, Scotland. TED video, 10:52, https://www.ted.com/talks/uri_alon_why_science_demands_a_leap_into_the_unknown.

Page 133 – O'Neil, Colin. *Protecting the Peel: Environmental Conservation in the Age of First Nations Self-government, an Examination of Conservation in Yukon's Peel Watershed*. Toronto: York University Library, 2017: 71. http://hdl.handle.net/10315/34271.

Page 136 – Harvey, Fiona. "Paris Climate Change Agreement: the world's greatest diplomatic success." *The Guardian,* Monday Dec 14, 2015. https://www.theguardian.com/environment/2015/dec/13/paris-climate-deal-cop-diplomacy-developing-united-nations.

Page 137 – Chan, Sewell. "On the Cusp of Climate History – But First Lunch." *New York Times*, December 12, 2015. https://www.nytimes.com/interactive/projects/cp/climate/2015-paris-climate-talks/cop21-speeches.

Page 138 – The University of Melbourne. "A Conversation with Nigel Topping." May 18, 2022. Video, 5:14. https://www.youtube.com/watch?v=-okNaKnQc0I&t=1s.

Page 138 – Champions-Speakers. "Exclusive Q&A with UK Climate Champion/ Nigel Topping on Corporate Strategy." https://www.youtube.com/watch?v=ICtoh5wlEPg&t=95s May 12, 2021 interview with Nigel Topping.

Page 139 – Carcross Tagish First Nation. "Book I and Book II." Accessed June 21, 2022. https://www.ctfn.ca/publications/legislation/book-i-ii/.

page 140 – Sutherland, Rory. "Life Lessons from an Ad Man." Filmed July 2009 in Oxford, England. TED video, 16:23, https://www.ted.com/talks/rory_sutherland_life_lessons_from_an_ad_man.

Page 140 – Ong, Walter. *Literacy and Orality*. New York: Routledge, 2002, 46-47.

Page 141 – Reconciliation Canada. "A Message from Chief Robert Joseph." Accessed September 29, 2017. http://www.reconciliationcanada.ca.

Page 142 – My notes from a speech hosted by Reconciliation Canada given by Chief Robert Joseph in Whitehorse, Yukon, November 3, 2016.

Page 143 – Birdsong, Mia. "The Story We Tell About Poverty Isn't True." Filmed May 2015 in Monterey, California. TED video, 15:08, https://www.ted.com/talks/mia_birdsong_the_story_we_tell_about_poverty_isn_t_true.

Page 144 – Liu, Yang and Kevin Passino. "Swarm intelligence: Literature Overview." Columbus: Ohio State University, 2000: 2. http://www.eleceng.ohio-state.edu/~passino/swarms.pdf.

Page 146 – McClellan, Catherine. *Part of the Land, Part of the Water: A History of Yukon Indians*. Vancouver: Douglas & McIntyre, 1987, 322.

Page 148 – Chongtham, Nirmala, Madho Bisht, and Sheena Haorongbam. "Nutritional Properties of Bamboo Shoots: Potential and Prospects for Utilization as a Health Food." *Comprehensive Reviews in Food Science and Food Safety* 10, no. 3 (2011): 153-168. https://onlinelibrary.wiley.com/doi/full/10.1111/j.1541-4337.2011.00147.x.

Page 149 – Hewlett, Sylvia Ann. "Too Much Testosterone on Wall Street?" *Harvard Business Review*. January 7, 2009. https://hbr.org/2009/01/too-much-testosterone-on-wall.

Page 149 – Tómasdóttir, Halla. "A Feminine Response to Iceland's Financial Crash." Filmed December 2010 in Washington, DC. TED video, 9:29, https://www.ted.com/talks/halla_

tomasdottir_a_feminine_response_to_iceland_s_financial_crash/

Page 150 Emmons, Robert A., Michael E McCullough. "Counting Blessings Versus Burdens: An Experimental Investigation of Gratitude and Subjective Well-being in Life." *Journal of Personality and Social Psychology*, vol 84, no. 2 (2003): 377-387.

Page 152 – Griggs, Tamar. "Parking Reprimand Leads to Love, Humour and Grace." *Gulf Islands Driftwood Newspaper*, November 29, 2017.

Page 153 – Bostrom, Nick. "What Happens When Computers Get Smarter Than We Are?" Filmed March 2017 in Vancouver, BC. TED video, 16:22, https://www.ted.com/talks/nick_bostrom_what_happens_when_our_computers_get_smarter_than_we_are.

Page 155 – Chung, Emily. "AI Must Turn Focus to Safety, Stephen Hawking and Other Researchers Say." *CBC News Science*, January 13, 2015. https://www.cbc.ca/news/technology/ai-must-turn-focus-to-safety-stephen-hawking-and-other-researchers-say-1.2899067.

Page 156 – NPR Invisibilia. "Raising Devendra." Accessed March 20, 2023. https://www.npr.org/2019/12/17/788681618/raising-devendra.

Page 156 – NPR Shortwave. "Can You Teach a Computer Common Sense?" Accessed March 20, 2023. https://www.npr.org/2023/01/30/1152568554/can-you-teach-a-computer-common-sense.

Page 158 – Kahane, Adam. *Power and Love: A Theory of Practical Social Change*. San Francisco: Berrett-Koehler Publishers, 2010: 12.

Page 159 – My interview with Dick Wittington April 11, 2014 in Vancouver.

Page 165 – Information board at the Mt Vesuvius excavation site viewed March, 2009.

Page 164 – AAA Foundation for Traffic Safety. "Prevalence of Self-Reported Aggressive Driving Behavior." Accessed April 1, 2016. http://newsroom.aaa.com/wp-content/uploads/2016/07/aggressive_driving_REPORT_7_14.pdf.

Page 164 – CBC Definitely Not the Opera. "Sook-Yin Lee Interview with Clare Lawlor: The Science of Revenge." Accessed July 22, 2017. http://www.cbc.ca/player/play/2295563704.

Page 165 – Oreskes, Naomi, and Erik Conway, *Merchants of Doubt: How A Handful of Scientists Obscured the Truth on Issues from Tobacco Smoking to Global Warming.* New York: Bloomsbury Press, 2010.

Page 165 – Kearns, Cristin, Laura Schmidt, and Stanton Glantz. "Sugar Industry and Coronary Heart Disease Research: A Historical Analysis of Internal Industry Documents." *JAMA Intern Med* 176, no. 11 (2016):1680-1685. https://jamanetwork.com/journals/jamainternalmedicine/fullarticle/2548255.

Page 165 – Domonoske, Camila. "50 Years Ago, Sugar industry Quietly Paid Scientists to Point Blame at Fat." NPR The Two Way, September 13, 2016. https://www.npr.org/sections/thetwo-way/2016/09/13/493739074/50-years-ago-sugar-industry-quietly-paid-scientists-to-point-blame-at-fat.

Page 166 – Centers for Disease Control and Prevention. "Adult Obesity Facts." Accessed May 25, 2022. https://www.cdc.gov/obesity/data/adult.html.

Page 167 – Webster, Joanne P. "The Effect of Toxoplasma Gondii on Animal Behavior: Playing Cat and Mouse." Schizophrenia Bulletin 33, no. 3 (2007): 752-756. https://academic.oup.com/schizophreniabulletin/article/33/3/752/1882250 .

Page 171 – Safian, Robert. "Terri Kelly: The 'Un-CEO' of W.L. Gore, on How to Deal with Chaos: Grow Up." *Fast Company,* 2012. https://www.fastcompany.com/3002493/terri-kelly-un-ceo-wl-gore-how-deal-chaos-grow.

Page 172 – Emergence Magazine. "The Serviceberry: An Economy of Abundance." Accessed December 5, 2020. https://emergencemagazine.org/essay/the-serviceberry/.

Page 173 – Alon, Uri. "Why Science Demands a Leap into the Unknown." Filmed June 2013 in Edinburgh, Scotland. TED video, 15:39, https://www.ted.com/talks/uri_alon_why_science_demands_a_leap_into_the_unknown.

Page 175 – Parry, Jacob. "Unlimited Vacation Time is Now a Reality at One Vancouver Startup." *BC Business Magazine,* Jan 14, 2016. https://www.bcbusiness.ca/unlimited-vacation-time-is-now-a-reality-at-one-vancouver-startup.

Page 175 – Christensen, Nathan. "We Offered Unlimited Vacation Time for One Year. Here's What We Learned." *Fast Company Magazine,*

November 2, 2015. https://www.fastcompany.com/3052926/
we-offered-unlimited-vacation-for-one-year-heres-what-we-learned.

Page 177 – Csikszentmihalyi, Mihaly. *Flow: The Psychology of Optimal Experience*. New York: Harper & Row, 1990.

Page 178 – Limb, Charles. "Your Brain on Improv." Filmed November 2010 in Washington, DC. TED video, 16:15, https://www.ted.com/talks/charles_limb_your_brain_on_improv/transcript.

Page 178 – CNBC Make It. "How This Former Sudanese Child Soldier was Inspired by P. Diddy." Accessed June 12, 2022. https://www.cnbc.com/video/2018/10/22/how-ex-sudanese-child-soldier-emmanuel-jal-became-a-hip-hop-artist.html.

Page 181 – CBC Tapestry. "Love in the Lab." April 26, 2019. https://www.cbc.ca/radio/tapestry/love-in-the-lab-1.5112420.

Page 181 – Goode, Erica. "Scientists Find a Particularly Female Response to Stress." *The New York Times: Section A,* May 19, 2020.

Page 182 – Zeidler, Maryse. "Custom-made Carts for Bottle-pickers Coming to Vancouver." CBC News, October 28, 2018. https://www.cbc.ca/news/canada/british-columbia/binner-project-carts-1.4878988.

Page 184 – James, Erwin. "The Norwegian Prison Where Inmates are Treated Like Humans." *The Guardian*, February 25, 2013. https://www.theguardian.com/society/2013/feb/25/norwegian-prison-inmates-treated-like-people.

Page 185 – Zoukis, Christopher. "Not the Worst, But Not Norway: US Prisons vs. Other Models." *HuffPost*, September 6, 2017. https://www.huffpost.com/entry/not-the-worst-but-not-norway-us-prisons-vs-other_b_59b0772ae4b0c50640cd646d.

Page 185 – Harris, Stefon. "There Are No Mistakes on the Bandstand." Filmed November 2011 in New York, New York. TED video, 12:25, https://www.ted.com/talks/stefon_harris_there_are_no_mistakes_on_the_bandstand.

Page 186 – Keats, Jonathon. "The Accidental Origins of an Outdoor Clothing Essential." Wired, January 14, 2018.

Page 187 – Emergence Magazine. "The Serviceberry: An Economy of Abundance." Accessed December 5, 2020. https://emergencemagazine.org/essay/the-serviceberry/.

Page 187 – Grossman, Mindy. "HSN's CEO on Fixing the Home Shopping Network's Culture." *Harvard Business Review* (December 2011): 42-46. https://hbr.org/2011/12/hsns-ceo-on-fixing-the-shopping-networks-culture.

Page 194 – Ong, Walter. *Literacy and Orality.* New York: Routledge, 2002: 24.

Page 195 – Sandberg, Sheryl. *"Lean In: Women, Work and the Will to Lead."* New York: Alfred Knopf, 2017: 82.

Page 196 – Notes from a Queen's University gathering in 2015 and interviews with Brent Bergeron, September 20, 2016 and Colin Joudrie, February 3, 2023.

Page 200 – Cain, Susan. *Bittersweet: How Sorrow and Longing Make Us Whole.* New York: Crown Publishing, 2022, 94.

Page 203 – Brown, Stuart. *Play: How it Shapes the Brain, Opens the Imagination, and Invigorates the Soul.* New York: Avery, 2009, 5.

Page 204 – Alon, Uri. "Why Science Demands a Leap into the Unknown." Filmed June 2013 in Edinburgh, Scotland. TED video, 15:39, https://www.ted.com/talks/uri_alon_why_science_demands_a_leap_into_the_unknown.

Page 205 – Brown, Stuart. *Play: How it Shapes the Brain, Opens the Imagination, and Invigorates the Soul.* New York: Avery, 2009: 15-21.

Page 206 – Brene Brown. "Unlocking Us: Brene with Scott Sonasheim on Why We Will Never be the Same (And Why it is Time to Talk About It)." Accessed April 2, 2022. https://brenebrown.com/podcast/why-well-never-be-the-same-again-and-why-its-time-to-talk-about-it-2/.

Page 207 – Brown, Stuart. *Play: How it Shapes the Brain, Opens the Imagination, and Invigorates the Soul.* New York: Avery, 2009, 233.

Page 209 – Barta, Thomas, Markus Kleiner, and Tilo Neumann. "Is There a Pay-off From Top-team Diversity?" *McKinsey Quarterly*, April 2012. https://www.mckinsey.com/business-functions/organization/our-insights/is-there-a-payoff-from-top-team-diversity.

Page 210 – Storvik, Aagoth. "Women on Boards – the Experience from the Norwegian Quota Reform." *Institute for Social Research, Oslo.* CESifo *Dice Report*, no. 1 (2011): 35-41. https://www.ifo.de/DocDL/dicereport111-rm2.pdf.

Page 211 – Tómasdóttir, Halla. "A Feminine Response to Iceland's Financial Crash." Filmed December 2010 in Washington, DC. TED video, 9:29, https://www.ted.com/talks/halla_tomasdottir_a_feminine_response_to_iceland_s_financial_crash/transcript.

Page 216 – Burkus, David. *Under New Management: How Leading Organizations are Upending Business as Usual.* HarperCollins Publishers Ltd., 2016.

Page 217 – Frampton, Sam. "How Zappos Customer Service Wows Customers." Chattermill, March 13, 2020. https://chattermill.com/blog/zappos-customer-service/.

Page 219 – My interview with Allison Rippin-Armstrong in Whitehorse, April, 2016.

Page 222 – Notes from Brent Bergeron's talk at the 2016 Prospectors and Developers Association of Canada conference in Toronto.

Chapter 6: Summary

Page 224 – Smith, Adam. *Wealth of Nations.* Ware, England: Wordsworth Editions, 2012.

Page 225 – Smith, Adam. *The Theory of Moral Sentiments (Cetakan 3).* Cambridge, New York: Cambridge University Press, 2005.

Acknowledgments

I'm always listening to find the meaning behind people's words and actions; I dwell on song lyrics and movie messages. As a result, there was a steady gift of inspiration from the people I encountered as this book took shape. My wish is that I have turned their generosity into another gift: something of everyday relevance to your life.

The Bridge is the product of a Fellowship through Simon Fraser University Centre for Dialogue. I deeply appreciate everyone there, especially Mark Winston, Laurie Anderson, Shauna Sylvester, Deb Harford and Sebastian Merz for their support of the 2 Ways of Knowing (2WK) Project. Silvia Heinrich and Michelle Eades joined the project at inception and were wonderful to work with. I am humbled by the years they helped foster the project into what it is today.

Workshop, speaking, and consultation work also supported the book writing. Thank you to Boucher Institute of Naturopathic Medicine, Jesse Duke Consulting, Casino Mining Corporation, SFU Executive MBA in Indigenous Business and Leadership, BC Chartered Accountants, the SFU Master of Education (MEd) in Contemplative Inquiry and Approaches in Education program, the Association for

Mineral Exploration BC and Queen's University Master of Earth and Energy Resources Leadership. An invitation from the UN Intergovernmental Forum on Mines, Minerals, Metals and Sustainable Development (IGF) to attend their annual general meetings was also a rich source of information and inspiration.

My experience with many geologists, land claims negotiators, business leaders, story structure analysts, and social workers, also informed this book.

My family were generous with their knowledge-sharing, especially Dave Joe, Lawrence Joe, Jesse Hudson, Jamie Joe-Hudson, Ignat Poltorasky, Dan Witt and Lori Hudson-Fish.

I am grateful to Elders and Chiefs who shared their wisdom, including Tommy Bosin-Smith, Joe Johnson, Harry Allen, Charles Eikland Sr, Bill Webber, Mark Wedge, Dave Keenan, James Allen, Patrick Van Bibber, Gerry Oldman, and Robert Joseph. They were all deeply inspiring. These personal experiences first brought me into contact with an active form of what I call circular thinking. At the same time, the ideas presented here are not presuming to represent another person's viewpoint, or Indigenous knowledge, in any way. I recount these stories to respect the time people took to explain their perspective to me and honor the inspirations that they initiated. I feel fortunate to have been offered these stories and teaching from which I have gleaned my own insights to share in this book.

Several people kindly agreed to be interviewed for this project and are named in this book with their surname. True stories that may cast an unflattering light on a person, yet offer great insights, are told using an imaginary first name (no surname) to prevent the slightest possibility of embarrassment. Unless, of course, if it is a story about me, in which case I'm happy if my embarrassment saves someone else's.

Lori Bamber did a substantive edit of the manuscript with elegant skill and generous support, especially in my moments of self-doubt. Trevor McMonagle provided his rigorous eye to the copy edit and Yicong Li provided fact checking services for which I am grateful. John Geddes, Laurie Anderson, Jesse Hudson, Kirk Cameron, Colin O'Neil, Brenda Morrison, and Laurel Parry offered their skills as readers. Their perspectives and expertise were invaluable to my efforts to create broadly relevant language for linear and circular thinking. The Starbucks in Whitehorse also has my gratitude. The management was uplifting in the way a kind and welcoming environment was created. It nourished me through countless hours of editing, especially during the Covid 19 years. Many friends debated with me and supported me over the years of writing and editing. I hope they all know how much I appreciate them.

This has been an epic journey and I sincerely thank all the people who have engaged with me along the way.

Author Biography

Kim is the Founder of the 2 Ways of Knowing Project (2wk), which she developed as a Fellow at Simon Fraser University Centre for Dialogue. Her work as an author, speaker, workshop facilitator, and consultant over the past 30 years has been with the mineral industry, film industry, and Federal, Territorial and several First Nation governments. Kim's experience as an exploration geologist, prospector, Yukon Water Board Member, Chair of the Yukon Land Use Planning Council, Federal Comprehensive Land Claims Negotiator, and mother have fueled her passion for pattern recognition. Kim calls the Yukon home and this is her second book. You can contact Kim at kimhudsonauthor@gmail.com or visit her site kimhudsonauthor.com.

Index

Printed in the USA
CPSIA information can be obtained
at www.ICGtesting.com
LVHW090120110724
785178LV00033B/494

9 781915 785015